Rock Island Public Library
401 - 19th Street
Rock Island, IL 61201-8143

S0-BRY-562

JUN 2007

Hooking Up:
You'll Never
Make Love
in This Town *Again*
Again

by Olivia, Carly, Amanda, and Jennifer

Copyright ©2006 Phoenix Books

All rights reserved. Written permission must be secured from the publisher to use or reproduce any part of this book, except brief quotations in critical reviews and articles.

ISBN: 1-59777-504-5
Library of Congress Cataloging-In-Publication Data Available

Book Design by: Sonia Fiore

Printed in the United States of America

Phoenix Books
9465 Wilshire Boulevard, Suite 315
Beverly Hills, CA 90212

10 9 8 7 6 5 4 3 2 1

Olivia

Early Years

I was born and raised in a small town in Minnesota. It was a rural upbringing: several main streets in town, winding two-lane roads, dairy farms dotting the outlying countryside. My parents were two small-town farm kids, high school sweet-hearts, when my mom found herself pregnant at the age of 15. They decided to get married because they had been raised religiously and both believed it was the right thing to do. On the day of my birth in April 1968 both of my parents had just turned sixteen. My brother followed when I was less than a year old. Mom and Dad were raising two kids before either one was old enough to vote or order a drink in a bar. They had to grow up fast.

When I was a kid most of my friends lived in big homes in suburban developments. Their fathers were doctors and local businessmen, and they all had stay-at-home moms. I was the exception because my mom worked. She was a hairdresser, and my dad was a truck driver. They were both hard workers and good providers, but as I grew up it never occurred to either parent that I should be making plans for the future. Higher education was not something that was ever discussed in our house. Of course, they hadn't had that opportunity themselves, and it didn't even cross their minds that they should try to prepare my brother or me for college. When my classmates and I all had to take SAT's in high school, I didn't even know what they were for or why I was taking them.

I was five foot ten by the ninth grade, with blonde hair and blue eyes I inherited from my Scandinavian father. I had a very fresh, all-American look and did some modeling jobs for department stores in Minneapolis from the time I was about 12. I appeared in local newspaper ads and had quite a few clips by the time I was a teenager. In high school I paid a local photographer to take some professional pictures of me, and the summer I was sixteen my mother and I hopped on a bus and traveled to New York City.

We stayed in a cheap hotel and took buses all over the city, cold-calling all the modeling agencies. I remember seeing Janice Dickinson on the cover of *Vogue* on every newsstand in New York that week. This was in the eighties, before the supermodel phenomenon took off and girls started making crazy money. I never thought I could make a fortune; I just thought being a model was cool. I signed with the Ford Agency and stayed with them for years, doing mostly catalog work. I knew I didn't want to live in New York, so I never got too serious about the profession. Really modeling was more of a lark. I always had a steady boyfriend; probably my parents assumed I would marry young and live a life similar to theirs in our hometown.

When high school graduation arrived I had no idea what to do with my life. Many of my friends were going to the local community college, and a few were headed off to state schools—but college had never seemed a likely option for me. I'd had no help or guidance at home or at school with applications, loans, any of that stuff. Seeing that I was somewhat aimless and adrift, my best friend and her divorced mother asked me if I wanted to accompany them to California, where they were relocating now that my friend had finished school. I didn't have any goals, money or plans, so I decided why not, and moved with them. We drove across the country. It was quite an adventure—outside of my one trip to New York, I had never been out of Minnesota before.

My girlfriend and her mom settled in an apartment in a quiet part of Ventura County, north of Los Angeles, and I enrolled in Ventura City College, still having no idea what I wanted to do with my life. Pretty much the only reason I even bothered to sign up and attend any classes was because I knew that's what all my friends back home were doing, and my friend's mother encouraged me to keep learning.

I found a part-time job at a local department store, the May Company. There was no way I could afford a car, so I rode my bike to work and school. After three months of this not-very-exciting new life, I had heard from the other kids at school that Santa Barbara was the "in" place to be, and one weekend I put myself on a Greyhound bus and went to check it out. I immediately loved it and knew this was where I was meant to live.

I was still in touch with my old high school boyfriend, who was a couple of years older than me, attending Minnesota State and not really loving it. His aunt died and left him a $15,000 inheritance, a pretty good sum back in those days. When he got the money, he immediately dropped out of school and we moved in together in a small apartment in Santa Barbara. We both found jobs. I worked at a Pappagallo shoe store—very trendy at the time—and took classes at Santa Barbara City College. My boyfriend waited tables at an upscale restaurant while he figured out what to do with his life.

The two of us blew through that $15,000 fast and had a lot of fun doing it. We both adjusted quite easily to the California lifestyle, to say the least. We made tons of new friends, rich college kids, and went out and had a great time with them every night of the week. We ate out every meal, drank and danced in all the Santa Barbara hotspots. But when I found out my boyfriend had cheated on me I dumped his ass in a hurry. I didn't need him—it was easy to see that I would be fine on my own in Santa Barbara.

Prince Charming

I found a new job at a fashionable beauty supply store/salon and moved into an apartment with one of my friends from work. That's when the partying really started. I was leading quite a wild little life. I started hanging out with a group of rich, beautiful college girls who were in Santa Barbara basically to have a good time for four years while their parents footed the bills. I became very close with a great girlfriend, Cathy. She and I we used to do Ecstasy and go out and just get crazy. That was back in the day when Ecstasy was still real, not cut with rat poison or who-knows-what like it is now. The two of us were inseperable and got into all kinds of trouble together all over Santa Barbara and Montecito. Cathy had somehow gotten her hands on a full helium tank from a dentist's office, and we used to take hits off it and ride around just laughing all night. We were both young, blond and beautiful...we got a lot of attention wherever we went.

On an impulse Cathy and I took a road trip to Palm Springs one weekend in her antique Jaguar. We checked into the Hilton, then got all dressed up and went out to find some fun.

The two of us were shaking it on the dance floor in a fancy nightclub when I caught his eye of an Armenian prince. I didn't realize he was a prince at that moment, of course—I just saw an old man beckoning us over to his table. He turned out to be a very nice man who ordered champagne and told us he'd like to take us both out for a meal the next day. We figured why not, it was harmless fun, and met up with him the next day. The three of us lounged around his hotel pool for awhile, then he took us out for a very lavish brunch at the best restaurant in Palm Springs.

I was still young and naïve—I'd only been out of Minnesota for a year. The prince was at least 55 years old, while I hadn't even turned 20. This man was immediately crazy about me; he presented me with an emerald bracelet at the end of the meal and asked me to stay in touch. He told me he would take me shopping whenever I wanted and to please call him soon—that he could always be reached at the number he gave me.

A week or so later I gave him a call, and during our conversation the prince invited me to go shopping in Newport Beach. He assured me that he'd put me up in a hotel. He booked me a beautiful room at the Hilton Newport, which made me feel safe when I arrived. Then off we went in his limousine to Neiman-Marcus and Saks Fifth Avenue and all kinds of private boutiques. I had never even been inside stores like that before. I was from the Midwest; I just wore regular clothes, from J.C. Penney's or the Gap. Maybe Lord and Taylor for a really big treat, the place my mom might put a coat on layaway for herself every few years. We certainly didn't have the means to buy a coat outright at Lord & Taylor.

I was more than dazzled. A whole new world of private shoppers and estate jewelry and $300 bottles of champagne was opening up in front of me. I didn't even know what to do that first trip; I didn't even know what to try on at such a fancy store. Eventually I chose four pairs of shoes and several outfits. Meeting the prince marked a very big turning point in my life. And it all seemed so harmless…he didn't try a thing that weekend. He didn't lay a hand on me or even try to kiss me. I went to sleep that night all alone in my fancy hotel room surrounded by Neiman-Marcus bags and wondered what this was all about. I knew he must want something from me, but he was a complete gentleman the entire weekend. So when he called and asked me to come visit again a couple weeks later, I jumped right into my little VW Bug and went.

I was afraid to actually have sex with him—he seemed so old!—but eventually we fooled around plenty. By fooling around I mean kissing, and he touched me all over, but I never had intercourse with him or even gave him a blow-job. I pretty much just let him touch me, and that seemed to be enough for him. I was learning quite a lot about the power of youth and beauty where older men were concerned. I found it very interesting, and a lot different than dating college guys: with older men, it's not always about penetration. Plenty of old rich guys just want to be around somebody pretty and young, a girl they can talk to and take out for meals and have fun with. Just having a young, gorgeous blond to amuse him and keep him company was enough for some men, and the Prince was one of them. He was willing to do a lot of nice things for me. Actual sex, I learned, was not always a requirement.

The Prince was a sweet older man—a real teddy bear. He was married with kids, of course, and maintained homes in Santa

Barbara, Palm Springs and Newport Beach. The whole relationship felt very strange to me, nothing I advertised to my girlfriends, but it went on for quite awhile. The main effect seeing this man had on me was to get me hooked on the finer things in life. As time passed the prince spent a fortune on me—shoes, outfits, jewelry, handbags—whatever I wanted was mine. I soon grew quite comfortable in the best stores and restaurants. We saw each other for a good year or so, whenever he was in town. He used his Santa Barbara house as a weekend place and saw me when he could get away from his family. Every time I saw him, he gave me money. And I was happy to take it.

That's how it all started. And when I look back on that time in my life I realize that any young girl could get sucked into that kind of situation.

Making Movies

My girlfriend Hayley, who lived up the street from me, asked me one day if I wanted to come with her to LA, where she was auditioning for a movie role. Why not? After Hayley read she told the casting agent, "My girlfriend drove down with me from Santa Barbara—you have to hear her read. She's really good." I had never acted a day in my life, but they asked me to read some lines. And apparently I *was* pretty good. I wound up being cast in a small part. I had a few lines, nothing big—I played a snotty private school girl.

Suddenly, within a week, I was off to Greece for a six-week shoot. I had to scramble around to get a passport. It was quite surreal to be nineteen years old and on a film set, surrounded by actors and producers and movie people. Joely Fischer and her sister Tricia were both in the movie; so was Patricia Arquette. All kinds of young actresses who went on to become quite well-known were in the cast of this little film. Joely, the daughter of Connie Stevens and Eddie Fisher, and I became great friends on the set—she was attending Boston University at the time as well as pursuing an acting career. (To this day I run into her in town and she couldn't be nicer—she still remembers me. What a lovely, down-to-earth woman.)

It never even occurred to me, after I got back from Greece, to start taking acting classes, look for an agent, start auditioning and networking. That would have been the smart move. I had become eligible for Screen Actors Guild membership because of my role in the movie, but I never bothered to pay my dues so I never received my SAG card and officially enrolled. I didn't have a manager or an agent or anyone advising me.

I didn't pursue acting as a career, because I just didn't have the skills to set goals, make plans, and go for them. I wasn't someone who had been dying to be an actress for years and was serious about the craft. Really, I had no idea what I wanted to do with my life, so I did what came easiest to me. For a young, blonde, beautiful girl on her own, you know what that is. I had already seen how easy it was.

What if.... What if my family had prepared me better for the world? What if I had had a real idea of who and what I wanted to be and was determined to make it happen? What if I had really studied acting and taken the industry seriously? Who knows if it would have stopped me from sleeping with men for money. We all do choose our destinies. Our choices choose our experiences, and our lives are what we make of them.

At the time, it didn't feel like I was closing any doors. Everything seemed like fun and good times.

My First Movie Star

I met Kevin Costner at the Blue Agave restaurant in Santa Barbara. I still had my regular job at the beauty supply store. I was 20 years old, in great shape, looking good, doing some modeling. I still took classes in Santa Barbara and had started to book a few modeling gigs in LA after the movie came out. At this time, the early nineties, Kevin was still married to his first wife Cindy. He and I saw each other across the crowded bar; I definitely noticed him noticing me. He was sitting alone, looking around, checking out all the women. He was certainly looking around for something.

I was with a bunch of girlfriends and decided to go for it. Finally I approached him. I didn't think it was going to go anywhere; I just thought it was fun to talk to a movie star. We laughed, talked, hung out for at least a couple of hours. I think it was easier for him to try to pick me up after a few drinks. He didn't have to try very hard—I was more than willing. Kevin was really nice and, of course, amazingly handsome. He was just so good-looking, and a huge movie star. I think he was in Santa Barbara on location for a film.

We kept on flirting and drinking, and eventually he invited me back to the hotel where he was staying, a very posh 5-star hotel in Montecito. I followed in my little VW bug. Of course we didn't enter the hotel together. I walked in separately a few minutes after he did. I took the elevator up to his suite, and stepped onto the set of a romantic movie.

It was a beautiful suite, and when I came in he took my hand and led me into the lavish bathroom. He knelt down and drew me a bath, complete with rose petals floating in the water. He kissed my body from head to toe. Kevin Costner was a fantastic lover. The sex was amazing. He was gentle and kind and we got along great. It wasn't awkward at all when the sex was over; he wasn't trying to get rid of me immediately and shoo me out the door or anything.

We just chatted about life. He never mentioned his work or his movies, ever. Not once. He asked about me and where I was from, what kinds of things I was interested in, what had brought me to California. It was like a date, honestly. And then I left. He gave me something when I left, for the life of me I can't remember what it was now, some kind of T-shirt with a film company logo or something. *And* he asked me for my phone number. I gave it to him and floated out of the hotel. I was walking on air. Waiting for his call.

I told all the girls where I worked about what had happened. I was so excited. It was sort of big news in town for a few days, that I had seen Kevin Costner. As the days passed, my girlfriends who had been with me that night at the Blue Agave tried to encourage me, saying, I'm sure he liked you, of course he's going to call you! All that kind of stuff.

I was truly heartbroken when he didn't call. I really thought we had connected; I actually thought this married movie star was going to call me! It was just a quick one-night stand for him. I'm sure he had forgotten me by the time he woke up the next morning and went to work.

Madam Alex

A girlfriend of mine named Tracy introduced me to one of her friends who lived down in LA. Tracy and I took a short road trip to visit her one weekend and I had so much fun at a nightclub called VOLA. The place was packed with lots of good-looking young Arab guys who were studying at Pepperdine. They were flocking around me, buying me the most expensive champagne in the place. I was immediately hooked on this nightlife. Santa Barbara was great, but this was a whole new level of decadent. I decided that LA was *the* place to be and found a place to live that very weekend. I was 21 years old.

I moved some stuff into a small apartment in Van Nuys in a 12-unit building and commuted back and forth to Santa Barbara, where I still kept a shared apartment. A girl named Coco lived next door to me, and one day I walked over to visit her and saw a dildo lying on her bed. I said, "Oh my God, what is that?" I was still that naïve, at age 21.

We got to be friends as time went on, and I eventually met her older boyfriend…he owned a mechanical auto body shop. Coco told me that he was married and she saw him once a week. She always looked great and had beautiful clothes and accessories. I admired Coco's look; she was very polished and poised. She had no job or visible means of support.

I was trying to boost my modeling career. One day as I was sitting at home recovering from a boob job, Coco knocked on my door and said, "Hey, do you want to go to London?" I said, "Why London, what's going on there?"

She said, "There's this lady I know, her name is Alex, and she sends girls to special places for special events. It's all very nice and classy. You'll have fun!" Coco reassured me that I didn't have to do much; I was tall and blonde with blue eyes and had been modeling for years. All she needed was a beautiful girl; the friend who had been scheduled to go on this trip had dropped out at the last minute. Coco brought me over to meet Madam Alex so I would feel reassured about the whole idea.

Madam Alex checked me out very carefully—my hands and feet especially. She inspected my manicure and pedicure and spoke to me for a long time, making sure I had good manners and was able to make conversation. I was young and wild, so why not? It would be another adventure, like the movie. As Coco and I left Alex's small house, I turned to my friend and said, "Let's go!" Coco replied, "Great, we're leaving tonight."

The Biggest Arms Dealer in the World

We jumped on a plane that very night and landed at Heathrow the next morning, where we were met by a limousine and taken to the Dorchester Hotel in London. There were Arabs all over the place; sheiks everywhere I turned. I got called to dinner with Adnan Khashoggi, though the name meant nothing to me at the time. It wasn't until many years later I realized exactly who he was and what he did. Of course it was very apparent that he was important; I could tell because of the way everybody at the table treated him. Everyone flattered him, deferred to him and laughed at all his jokes, hanging on his every word.

At that dinner I was introduced to all kinds of high-ranking diplomats from various European countries. I was 21 years old, sitting there having dinner with royalty...I look back on that trip and think, *If I only knew then what I know now.* I must have seemed like such a little girl. Dumb, naïve, inexperienced...I had no idea who these people were sitting around me. I wish I had been able to speak to my dinner companions more intelligently, but I was so young. I have to wonder what those people thought of me.

Coco and I shared a room right down the hall from Adnan's Khashoggi's fancy suite. A day or so into our London stay, an envelope was delivered to our room. It was stuffed full of cash. That night, after another lovely dinner, Coco and I were summoned down the hall. I wasn't at all afraid; Adnan was kind and soft-spoken and adorable. My first time with an arms dealer— at 21 years old. I was on a high; it was a real rush getting that money. After Coco and I split the cash, it came to a few thousand dollars for being there just that one night. The sex was fine—nothing memorable or special.

We got a call in our room the next morning from Madam Alex. She didn't want us to return to LA quite yet...she said, "I've got two gorgeous Arab boys who are sons of the President of Saudi Arabia in Switzerland. What do you say?" I said yes! We jumped on a plane to Gstaad, one of the hottest and most exclusive places in the world to ski. I had such a good time with these two sons. Both were young, good-looking and polite. It was all very simple—honestly, they didn't seem too experienced. We just had basic, missionary-style sex. Nothing kinky or anything that lasted all day long. It was quite easy, and soon enough I was heading home with an envelope containing five grand in cash. I thought, *I don't want to work at I. Magnin department store anymore!* I quit the minute I got back home—just called and never went back. Madam Alex and I stayed in touch.

Marcus Allen

Football star Marcus Allen was a prominent resident of Santa Barbara back in those days. This was back in the 90's when he was known primarily as OJ's best friend—well before he became known because of the infamous murder, of course. Marcus had an affair with Nicole Brown Simpson and had all kinds of girlfriends. He also used to hire call girls all the time. I know, because he hired me.

He lived in a gorgeous mansion in Montecito. Once Marcus saw you professionally and liked you, he wanted you to keep coming back. I knew a couple of girls who saw him professionally, and they all told me the same thing. He liked to build a relationship with his call girls. That's just what happened with me. The first time I met him, we got right to it. But after he called me back, we would hang out, just like we were on a regular date. We used to sit in his living room and sip wine and listen to music; he would always offer to take me out to dinner or dancing. But I was very afraid to do that; Santa Barbara is a small community and I had no desire to be seen out in public with him.

It was always very romantic. He was always sweet and passionate. I saw him three times, but I could see that he really wanted something more than I was willing to give. I was after the rush, the big money, the good times, not someone who wanted a pseudo-girlfriend. I moved on.

Michael Jordan

I met Michael Jordan in Santa Barbara too. Santa Barbara/
Montecito is quite the happening place, a lot of stars and movie
people and athletes live there. For goodness' sake, even Oprah
lives there now. It's always been a magnet for celebrities.

Some girlfriends and I were out at another trendy nightclub,
drinking and having fun. I was wearing tons of makeup and a
miniskirt with high heels, as was the fashion back then. I
couldn't help but notice Michael Jordan and his posse—it was
huge. He must have had ten guys around him. I could feel him
looking at me across the room, but there was no way he was
going to approach me himself. He had one of his dudes make
the initial contact.

One of the guys approached our table and invited us all back
to the hotel where they were staying. We said sure, and followed them back. Michael Jordan and Company had taken
over an entire floor of the hotel. There were guys coming in
and out of different rooms, girls darting in and out of this
room and that room; it was quite a busy scene. I ended up with
Michael, as I knew I would. He had the most beautiful smile,
and what a kisser. Unbelievable.

Michael Jordan was fun. We had an all-night lovemaking session, and it was great. He was very passionate and intense, and
of course he is so handsome and in such amazing shape. I was
afraid he might be a little rough, given how big he was, but he
was gentle and affectionate. He rubbed my back and everything. I was his kind of girl: blond, voluptuous, blue eyes. I
knew who he was, of course, but I was so not into basketball. I
had no idea what team he played for, even. It was quite

embarrassing, all the talk was about basketball, he kept naming players from my hometown team and I had no idea what the hell he was talking about. He chuckled and gave up. "Sorry, I'm not really into basketball," I told him. He didn't care.

Everyone wants to know, how big was his dick? Well, it was big, but not gigantic. There are plenty of guys who are short and skinny and have those freaky huge penises that will surprise you. I'd had a boyfriend who wasn't any taller than 5 foot 8 who had the biggest dick I ever saw. You just never know. MJ was definitely well-endowed, but nothing freaky. I liked it just fine. He was perfect.

The funniest thing was when I left, I got a parting gift. As I was walking out the door at 9 the next morning, one of his guys called after me, "Hey, wait a minute, I've got something for you." I lingered in the hallway for a minute while he ran into a room and grabbed something. He handed me a box and I went out to my car and opened it. It was a pair of Air Jordan tennis shoes. And they were the right size! I laughed my head off the whole way home from the hotel. I couldn't believe it.

Stephanie

I still went out with girlfriends and on dates, booked modeling jobs, shuttled back and forth between L.A. and Santa Barbara and even took some classes. I had lots of fun times—like with Michael Jordan—but the lure of being a professional call girl started sucking me in more and more. The obscene amount of cash I could earn for what was usually a very luxurious quick trip abroad or fancy dinner "date" with often very attractive rich men was more than I could resist. Several years into this life, I met a girlfriend out on a job. I was called for a "date" and walked into a restaurant, and when I was escorted to the table there was an old friend of mine sitting there with a bunch of men. I'd known her family for years. I almost fainted. She could tell I was very freaked out and said reassuringly, "Sit down, it's OK. I'm here too!"

But I was so embarrassed, I could have died. I never wanted her to know. She knew my old boyfriends, I thought it would get back to my ex, all kinds of thoughts ran through my mind. I drank as much wine as I could and we headed upstairs to do our job. To meet a friend that you've known a long time in that situation is a very strange sensation to say the least. And what a situation—they had booked two girls, because that was always the most popular male fantasy. I had gotten used to three-ways and performing with other girls—mostly, it was all a show to turn men on—but this was a good friend!

Stephanie is the blondest, sweetest, most all-American girl you can imagine. We had sex together that night and many times since then. We had to—it was our job. After that first time we used to meet guys all the time together, both in Santa Barbara and L.A. In fact, we used to hang out together in an Italian restaurant on Pico in West L.A. whose clientele was mainly a bunch of Mafia guys. There was a hotel right next to the restaurant, which was very convenient. The two of us did great business.

Heidi Fleiss and Charlie Sheen

Heidi Fleiss started her "career" working for Madam Alex; rumor was she actually stole Alex's black book with all the numbers and went into business for herself. That's how all of Hollywood started using Heidi. I certainly didn't tell Madam Alex that I had met her arch-enemy and that someone else was going to be sending me on jobs. Because Alex did send me on a lot of things and I liked her, even though she took she took 40%.

When I met her, in the mid-nineties, Heidi lived in a house behind the Beverly Hills Hotel. A girlfriend took me up to the Roxy nightclub one night, where Heidi used to host a private gathering upstairs on certain nights. Heidi took a liking to me right away. She had some cocaine, and we went back to her house and started partying. Heidi was very hard to get to know; I didn't feel like I could open up to her or we would ever become very close. She had a masculine sort of energy about her; she could be very harsh and brassy.

She said, "Come see me tomorrow," and the very next day she sent me on a trip to Las Vegas to see some Arabs. Arabs were a big part of the business back then; they were the bread and butter of Madam Alex's business. They were all princes and sheiks, and they had tons of money to throw around. They were excellent clients for a working girl—they didn't have time to fuck and suck all day long. And they never got sappy and asked things like, "What's a nice girl like you..." They wanted to have a good dinner, mingle and talk with their friends, then go into their rooms and get it done. I started working for Heidi frequently, though I didn't care for her manner, which never warmed. She was very demanding about the way she went about things. I certainly didn't think I needed to be told how to style my hair or how to speak to clients.

There was a hip hotel called the St. James, right next to Rande Gerber's Skybar, the hottest bar in LA at the time. One day

Heidi called me because she wanted me to meet someone there. The client turned out to be Charlie Sheen, hanging out with a couple friends of his watching a basketball game on TV. Heidi had asked me to stop by just to meet him; Charlie liked to meet girls ahead of time to see if he was attracted to them. I sat around his suite for a couple hours, chatting and drinking some beers. When I left I wasn't sure if he had liked me or not—the situation had been a little awkward. I didn't know what to talk about, as I was still not a big basketball fan.

I was surprised when he called me the following weekend and invited me to his place in Malibu. I drove to his place, which was beautiful, of course. He had some friends over and we were all playing pool and drinking and having a good time. That's how it started…after that initial visit I saw him at least once a week for more than a year. He used to give me $1500 cash every time I saw him. We had a little fling; he used to take me on mini-vacations, to Palm Springs and to spas. Charlie was very generous, he gifted me with a vintage Rolex watch. I really fell for him; I wanted him to be my boyfriend for real. But when we got back from a long-weekend getaway, he didn't call me for a month, and I was devastated. I couldn't figure out what was going on.

One night I was sitting on my couch at home watching *Entertainment Tonight* and learned that Charlie had gotten married to a model. I was brokenhearted. I cried and called all my girlfriends. Look, I was naïve…I was not the only girl he was seeing, and probably not the only girl he gave gifts to. I later found out a lot of girls around town had vintage Rolexes—one of them belonged to a good friend of mine named Lisa! I had thought I was special, but I wasn't. He had my heart, but didn't want it. Still, he was so charming…to this day it gives me a little pang just to watch him on a TV show. I never saw him again. He did call me a couple times, after his first very short-lived marriage hit the rocks, but I refused to see him. I was too hurt.

Look, cheating was the reason his second marriage to Denise broke up. He's always going to be that kind of guy, he'll never change. Even ten years later, I felt sorry for her when they finally split for good because I'm sure she loved him; he's a very lovable guy. But he was a star, and stars think they can do whatever they want. In the end, this is why Denise left him. She caught him with a call girl. He got busted, that's all there is to it—I know it for a fact. Charlie Sheen will never get girls out of his system; he is not a one-woman man. There is no way he will ever be a faithful husband, to anyone. It's who he is; he's never going to change.

Laurence Fishburne

I had a rendezvous with Laurence Fishburne around this time. I used to see him in LA whenever he was in town—he used to get a hotel room and I'd go visit him. I met him at a party and he really liked me. He told me he was single, in the process of divorcing his wife, and we got along well, so I went to New York to visit him a couple of times.

This, like Kevin Costner or Michael Jordan, was not a paying situation. For many years I continued my "double life"—I made a lot of money as a call girl and booked lots of jobs through various madams, but at the same time I kept up my modeling career and went on dates and had boyfriends like a "regular" girl. The men I liked and really wanted to date or have a relationship had no idea what I did on the side.

He wasn't a "client," but Laurence did some nice things for me—he took me shopping and bought me lots of clothes and jewelry. He paid for sex, just not with cash. We were supposedly "dating," and I was supposedly the only one in his life. That was a lie.

I liked him a lot, but he was leading me on. He took me on a trip to New Orleans and we enjoyed a five-course meal at Emeril's followed by drinks at a jazz bar. We used to go out to dinner all the time—then fuck all night in his hotel room. One day, he just stopped calling me. I read in the tabloids that he had reconciled with his wife.

Rick James

For a brief time I shared an apartment in L.A. with a girl who was dating the drummer for Rick James. His name was Spider. Rick James was really something. He used to follow me around trying to get me to do cocaine. We hung out and had a good time, but he never paid me for sex. I didn't meet him on that level. He was a cool guy, but in those days he was in a complete drug haze. He wouldn't leave me alone. Underneath, he was really insecure; he needed constant validation. He liked a lot of compliments; his ego needed shoring up all the time.

I really think that a lot of celebrities who pay for sex are actually very insecure men deep down; they must feel they need to pay for sex in order to validate themselves. I think they're too scared and lazy to really get out there and pursue a woman. Hey, they can pay for it, why put themselves out there and risk any rejection. They're very egotistical.

(I ran into Rick years later, about a year before he died, at a doughnut shop on Melrose. We laughed when we saw each other, because we were both driving the same car—a Jeep Cherokee. Ahh, the good old days.)

Ava's Nightclub

The whole Charlie Sheen episode really took the wind out of my sails, but after few days' moping and crying I called Heidi, because I wanted to get the whole thing out of my system. And that's how I met Dan Aykroyd. He was married of course, to a wonderful woman who was a real beauty. Dan was really a lackadaisical guy, quick in bed, but I loved hanging out with him because he was very sweet. A big teddy bear. It was the same thing every time I saw him; nothing fancy. Wham, bam, thank you ma'am. I'm not sure what he was looking for...all these guys certainly could have gotten laid anytime. I think he, like most of my clients, just wanted someone to do things that their wives wouldn't...like talk dirty.

Dan was only a client briefly, but every little bit helped. I needed money constantly. Being a professional call girl required quite a lot of expensive upkeep. I had to go to the gym every day, get my nails done every week, my hair colored and constantly styled.... At the time having big lips was the latest look, so I used to go get injections at the plastic surgeon's office. Guys loved them sliding over their cocks.

Around this time Ava's nightclub opened in the Beverly Center, and boy, did that go over big with the working girls in town. That's pretty much all that was ever in that club—Mafia guys and some working girls, with a sprinkling of celebrities. The reason that I got invited to the opening was because Ava was a neighbor—she lived down the street from me on Burton Way in Beverly Hills. Ava was a former Playboy Bunny/call girl, one of Jerry Buss's girls. Jerry Buss was well-known around L.A. as a rich real estate developer who owned the Los Angeles Lakers and had quite a few lady friends. I didn't ask too many questions about where Ava got the money to open her own club. It had to have been from either Jerry Buss or one of her Mafia boyfriends in New York. I assumed someone must have fronted her the money in trade. No way someone's going to open a beautiful nightclub for you and not want any pussy.

The club was fantastic—the food was great, the dance floor was rocking, it was like Nipper's Nightclub all over again. Opening night was like Who's Who in Hollywood. New York Mafia guys, movie stars, you name it. Ava actually took me out to dinner one night with a big New York Mafia guy named Joe Dante; he died a few years ago from a heart attack. Joe Pesci was at our table—he was a nice guy, a bunch of us went over to his house one night. He picked who he wanted in his room; there were three girls at his house that night, and we all went into his room separately. Joe had sex with each one of us that night, one right after the other.

I started stopping by Ava's nightclub every Friday night to see what celebrity was coming in. My girlfriends and I loved it there and used to go there all the time. Sadly, Ava's nightclub only lasted for about a year; I think that one of the guys who had put up the money got in some trouble over the liquor license and wound up serving time. That was the end of that, but they were good times while they lasted.

Arnold Schwarzenegger

I moved on to the bar in the Peninsula Hotel in Beverly Hills; it was where all the girls in town went to find guys for the night. It was the ideal place to meet rich older men. The Peninsula is a 5-star resort with gorgeous rooms and impeccable service, always a big favorite among actors and Hollywood people. And the bar in that hotel was call girl city. It was an open secret in L.A.: a man could always find a call girl at the Peninsula Bar. And there were always plenty of famous people lounging around there too; it made for a very happening scene.

I was hanging out with a bunch of girls there one night; we were the guests of some Arab prince. The Bar is set up like a luxurious living room with sofas and armchairs and lamps, very conducive to private conversations and cozy meetings. I was sitting on a couch drinking and laughing when I noticed that Arnold Schwarzenegger was seated just a few feet away on an adjoining couch, surrounded by business-type men. They looked like agents and managers. I got up and walked slowly past him to the bathroom, taking my time, making sure he noticed me. When I returned to my seat we started chatting back and forth a little bit.

After some flirting and eye contact he passed me a written note on a napkin. "Meet me up in my room." It was the Terminator, for God's sake, he was a huge movie star at the time, at the height of his fame. I knew he was married, of course, to Maria Shriver, but I didn't care. His body was amazing. I didn't care about getting paid either; I just went for it.

And damn, that man looked good naked. That's what I most remember about Arnold. This wasn't a paying situation, we just had a good time. It was another wild and crazy night. I had a lot of them back in the nineties.

Jean-Claude Van Damme

Being a call girl was big business in Los Angeles. Besides Madam Alex and Heidi, there were these two other ladies in town. They were Mexican women named Rose and Sophia, who pretended to be sisters. They were madams, successful ones, and I did some work for them.

Ordering two girls at once to put on a show was always a big favorite. I used to team up with a woman named Miriam all the time. She was a gorgeous brunette who claimed to be 27. It bugged me; I knew very well she was 37. Rose and Sophia used to send us places together all the time, because we were both tall with similar voluptuous bodies but exactly opposite in coloring; she was dark and I was blond. We were a very popular duo.

Miriam and I did all kinds of things together; once we went to Miami together on a yacht. That yacht must have been worth millions and millions of dollars. It was all cherrywood inside, the most luxurious thing I had ever seen. It was owned by a multi-billionaire Saudi Prince. The Prince was hosting a big important gathering with all kinds of his friends invited. There were ambassadors, other princes, European royalty—you name it; the who's who of the world all showed up on this yacht in Florida. And guess who was there and got seated at the table right next to me? Adnan Khashoggi. He didn't remember me, of course, this was years after our encounter. But our host, the Prince, got very annoyed because Adnan and I we were talking, laughing and getting along quite well. I could hardly say to the man who was paying me, "Hey, cool it, I've been with this guy before…I know him from London!" The Saudi Prince was so annoyed that he sent me home the next day to punish me for flirting with Khashoggi. Hey, he had told me to mingle with the guests!

Rose and Sophia called me one night about teaming up with Miriam for a date at the Peninsula Hotel. I had no idea who the client was, they made it a policy to never mention if the client was a celebrity before sending girls out. So I arrived and was sitting at a table in the bar with a bunch of girls and a few bodyguard-type guys. All of a sudden Jean-Claude Van Damme walked up to us. We all sat there drinking for awhile in the bar, then moved the party up to the room. He was on his second wife at the time. You know, that man was always married to someone, but it never seemed to slow his partying down.

There was one hell of a party going on in that suite. There was marijuana and alcohol and girls, girls, girls. I wound up in the bedroom with Jean-Claude; everyone else continued the party outside in the living room. We had wild sex. He was quite buzzed. Crazy fun sex—nothing soft or romantic here. It was all bend over this way and stand over there….Very athletic. He was in incredible shape, very fit. I stayed with him till at least 3 in the morning. He didn't want me to leave, but I was feeling antsy. I just didn't want to spend the night. Seeing that I was determined to leave, Jean-Claude told me that he had the room reserved for two days, that he was going out the following day but wanted me to come back the next night. He told me just to hang out in his room and wait for him to come back.

I went home very late that night but started calling the room the next afternoon. I called and called the room because I wasn't sure exactly what to do; I did have the room key but was nervous about just showing up. It turned out he had checked out! Ha. Those movie stars. But I kept that room key for the longest time; I thought it was cool.

Brad Pitt

I had plenty of business from the various madams in town, but on a whim one day I placed an ad in a local newspaper called *LA Express*. It was a rather raunchy publication with all kinds of risqué ads in the back pages. My ad didn't have a picture—it just said, HOT GIRL, HOT MASSAGE and then listed my cell phone number. I got a lot of business from that ad. Believe me, no one ever wanted a massage. I was still under 30 and really in great shape. I took excellent care of myself in many ways. I exercised every day, was a vegetarian, always had my hair and nails done and makeup on, though back then I really didn't even need it. I partied hard, too, but I really cared about my appearance. Any damage that came from too much drinking or cocaine hadn't affected my looks.

Wherever I went, I never had anyone say, "Sorry, you're not what I'm looking for," and send me home. Well, there was just one time, where I was just too tall. The client was tiny, and he had little man's complex—he didn't like me towering over him. I told him height didn't matter when we were lying down. He laughed, gave me a hundred bucks for cab fare and sent me home. Then he went looking for someone more petite who didn't threaten him.

One night I was drinking and partying pretty hard with some girlfriends when my cell phone rang and a male voice asked me if I would consider coming out to Malibu that night for a massage. I was broke, again—I made plenty of money but spent even more. Clothes, jewelry, partying...I had nothing better to do; so I said sure. I poured myself into a cab for the long ride out to the beach.

It's a long trip all the way out to Malibu—and I was wasted by the time we got to our destination. Back in those days I used to take some coke with me in my purse so I could do a couple quick lines in the client's bathroom—it made things a little easier to get through. I did a few lines of cocaine in the car on the way over. I was really flying high that night. The cab wound through the mountains of Malibu and stopped in front of a small house in the canyon. A man stood waiting on the front porch—he looked familiar. No way, couldn't be, but sure enough as I drew closer I realized it was Brad Pitt. Boy, did my heart start pounding.

This was back before his relationship and subsequent engagement to Gwyneth Paltrow, but he was already a huge movie star. He was also a real gentleman, and it was a quick businesslike call. We got right to it. Nothing romantic, nothing kinky. The guy just wanted to get off. He put on a condom and the whole thing was over pretty quick. He had a cone-shaped penis. Normal-sized, not particularly big, but it was certainly unusual. I had never seen a cone-shaped cock before. Being so high made the whole night feel particularly surreal. I did another line in the bathroom after we were finished. I told myself, "I'm in Brad Pitt's bathroom right now," as I leaned over and snorted. It was like a dream. A quick dream—I was in and out of that house in under an hour.

He was just a guy who wanted to get laid with no hassles. Very politely, he walked me outside to catch my cab back to town. He asked me for my number, said he wanted to see me again. Never heard that one before. Brad handed me $500 cash, then stood on the porch and waved as I stepped into the cab. I turned around and looked out the back window as we pulled away. He stood alone, watching the cab pull away. It was just like a movie.

The Woman Producer

A girlfriend and I had just finished seeing a client together when Rose and Sophia called me one day. Rose said, "I want you to meet this woman, she's in Hawaii right now, here's the number, give her a call." So I called up this woman, and she wound up inviting me to come to her house back in L.A. I had no idea when we talked that she was a movie producer who was divorced from another producer who had done some of the biggest movies of all time. Eventually I drove up to her house in the Hollywood Hills and spent the weekend with her. She was hard as nails and had a very serious cocaine habit, but she wanted me to stick around, so I decided to stay for awhile and see what developed. Having woman clients was unusual, but not unheard of. I'd done it before.

Soon things started getting weird. What a piece of work. Besides spanking and bondage, I soon learned that this woman liked girls to piss and shit on her. I lived at her place for about three weeks, and that kind of stuff didn't start right away, of course. Our relationship had been going along fine, very regular sex, lots of playacting, nothing special. She sort of eased me into what she really wanted. One day she asked me to piss on her in the shower, and I thought, *OK, sure, why not?* Then she asked me to shit on her. I really hesitated...and she said,

"Listen, I'll give you this much money." It was a ridiculous amount. So I shit on her, and she started eating it. That was way too much for me to handle; I knew I had to get out of there.

That night I thought, *It's definitely time for me to go; I am not into this kind of stuff.* But I can't lie; I did it a couple other times, for a lot of money. This rich, talented woman who had once done some great things in the film business liked nothing better than to lie in her beautiful marble bathtub, freebase cocaine and eat shit. She loved it. Hard to believe, but true. I thought that it would get easier—and it seemed like it would be easier than getting screwed by some guy in every hole for five straight hours—but it was just too weird and out-there. All that kind of talk… "Oooh, aaahhh…eat my shit! I'm going to piss on your face!" That's the kind of thing she wanted to hear.

I'm telling you, any working call girl could win an Academy Award any day for the acting they have to do. Any one of us is a better actress than Michelle Pfeiffer, who was rumored to have been in the business herself back in the day. She certainly did some things in the beginning of her career; she was no angel when she was starting out. All I know is you have to be a very talented actress to do this kind of work, because much of the time it's all about pretending to enjoy something you don't.

Because being a call girl is not like having sex with someone you'd choose to be with. I never counted having sex with clients as *really* having sex. When you're with someone you want to be with, it feels good. Charlie Sheen was the exception to the rule—I grew to love him. Someone like Dan Aykroyd was just a client, pure business. Because the dialogue a call girl has to come up with is just too much. "Oh yeah, lick my titties…"—it has to sound real, like you're really in the throes of excitement.

It takes practice, believe me. Because these guys want to hear… "Oh God, I thought about your cock last night; I can't wait for you to put in my cunt…" Bottom line, this is what they're paying you for. To tell them how big and hard their cock is. "Oh… you lick my pussy so good… I'm going to come all over your face…" I would say 97% of men want to hear talk like this, whether they're paying for it or not. Dirty talk; men love it.

I was too grossed out to continue watching this crazy woman eating my shit. I couldn't believe this was what I had resorted to in order to have some money. Well, the reality is that that's what I *was* doing. I returned to LA and tried to put the whole incident out of my mind.

Jack Nicholson

The phone was always ringing…the same girlfriend who introduced me to Dan Aykroyd called one day and asked me if I wanted to accompany her to Jack Nicholson's house. Jack was definitely a paying customer…my girlfriend had a regular thing going with him. She was beautiful, looked just like a Playmate, and saw him frequently. She used to go over to his house and do coke with him all the time.

The two of us drove up to his huge house on top of Mulholland Drive and got totally wild. We sat around his gorgeous mansion naked at his dining room table and did tons of blow and drank and just had a crazy time. I was a little worried—Jack had a well-publicized relationship going on with a model, Rebecca Broussard, at the time, and I sure didn't want her walking in on this scene. My girlfriend and I were giving him blow-jobs, putting on shows for him…you name it. Anything went. "Relax," he said, "she never comes down here." Apparently she had her own separate home where she lived with their kids.

Good thing too, because Jack Nicholson was just nuts. And I say that in a nice way. Kooky, funny, out of his mind. The whole thing was such a trip, because he was just so famous. I couldn't believe the things we were doing. I thought it was the coolest thing in the world. It was fun. Plus he paid us $1000 each. I accompanied my girlfriend there several times, but then she ran into a bit of trouble. She was Canadian, and had a fake green card from Joe Dante. She went home for a visit and when she tried to get back into the country, she was busted by Immigration for using false papers. That was the end of that. The two of us had always gone to his house together; I had never thought to get his number for myself. I was sorry; Jack was a lot of fun.

Marriage and Motherhood

The nineties were passing, quickly. I was getting older and starting to think about settling down a bit. I still modeled every now and then and made OK money, but a billboard in Germany or a catalog shoot meant working only a couple days out of the week. I could always land some kind of modeling gig, but looks and trends change over time. There was a time when blonde and voluptuous was in; there was time when heroin chic was in. My looks didn't always go with the times. And the easy money was always there in the call girl system.

At the time I met the father of my children, he was a top model who had done tons of commercials and was looking to break into acting. I had no doubt that he was well on his way to becoming the next Tom Cruise. I met my husband on a Lands End catalog shoot and we started dating. It became serious quickly. He certainly never knew I was a call girl—I mean, come on, he never even realized my boobs weren't real. I continued to see clients. We were only dating, after all, and I kept my own apartment and my own life.

The guy was great-looking, obviously, and he seemed to have his career together. I saw him on TV every night in one commercial or another. He had top designers like Versace flying him over to Italy to do his shows. He lived in a beautiful four-bedroom condominium on the West Side of L.A. and had a brand-new car he'd paid cash for. He certainly seemed like Prince Charming from a fairy tale.

One day we got into a big fight. I flew off to New York—I knew he would be following a couple of days later for a job he had booked. I had a big gig in Atlantic City with a girlfriend for a bunch of guys throwing a bachelor party. They were paying us really big money for a two-girl act. After my gig I joined my boyfriend at his hotel room in New York and we discussed our relationship and where it was going. We took a long walk through the streets of the city, and just as we were passing Tiffany he asked me, "What kind of ring would you want if I asked you to marry me?" I stopped at the window and said, "*That* kind, an emerald with two baguettes on the side!" And that's what I got, the very next day. He also presented me with five different credit cards—all gold and platinum—with my name on them, just so I would feel secure. We married shortly thereafter, and I resolved to give up being a call girl for good. It was time to try a new kind of life.

I immediately got pregnant and we were very happy for a while. My husband was generous, and we always had a good time together. We bought great clothes, spent money like water, went out to eat every night, took trips, had a darling baby and a nanny who came every day. He treated me very well. Life was picture-perfect for a couple of years.

I figured that whole part of my life—being a call girl—was done. No way was I ever going to do that again. At times I was tempted though, I can't lie. A girl named Liz called me one night and asked me to come see her. I met her over at a very trendy little flower store/restaurant called Rita Flora on La Brea in Hollywood, where she took my picture and chatted with me for a bit. She was looking for girls to send to Brunei. She also asked me if I had any friends who might be interested.

I had a girlfriend who would be perfect—Candy was her name—so I arranged an introduction. I was married with a baby—I couldn't take off to Brunei for three months. A big part of me really wanted to go. In fact, I thought for a good while about how I could make it all work, but it just wasn't going to happen. Several of my friends wound up going, Candy included. She called me a few times from Brunei, and after ninety days had passed she called to tell me, "I'm staying for another three months."

Candy was gone for a total of six months. They gave her $75,000 worth of Bulgari jewelry for her birthday. $50,000 in cash to go shopping with in London. This, on top of what she was already being paid! The money was absolutely crazy…I did envy that part of it, but I was happy in my life, so how could I really be jealous? I told myself to put it all out of my mind.

Falling Apart

My husband was on top of the world, but it all went to his head. He got very arrogant and thought he was more important than he really was. He wound up in a nasty lawsuit with his modeling agent, which was the kiss of death to his career. Filing that suit was such a bad idea—I begged him not to do it. There are plenty of models in the world, after all, and I couldn't believe suing one of the most powerful agents in the business could lead to anything but trouble. It didn't.

Getting older and losing your power is a real hazard in the modeling world—it eventually happens to most. It's especially hard on guys. My husband was making a couple of hundred thousand dollars a year off just one commercial—he really thought he was invincible. It was incredible how fast everything went bad after he lost his lawsuit. He started snapping all the time and picking on me, which quickly escalated into terrible verbal abuse. When I got pregnant for the second time, he really lost it.

I remember the day it hit me that our life together had gone terribly wrong. Our baby boy was fussing in his crib and I was trying to soothe him. I wasn't feeling great myself as I was eight months pregnant. My husband, meanwhile, was lounging in bed, refusing to get up for a catalog shoot. "My day rate is $2500 and I'm not getting out of bed for $750 for a half-day. I don't work half-days!" I couldn't believe it. "We have a baby to feed and $750 pays for plenty of groceries. What are you doing—this is no time for picking and choosing!" He'd always had a healthy ego, of course, but this was ridiculous. Money was power to him—and he had grown accustomed to having plenty of both. He didn't know what to do when it all started to crumble. He decided to sell the condo—something else I begged him not to do—and live on the cash until he could decide what his next move should be.

His next move was to fall apart. Sleep in till eleven o'clock every morning. Ignore everything, refuse to face the facts. We started to argue all the time, especially after the new baby arrived. One night he hit me, and the next thing I knew I was staying at my nanny's house in a one-bedroom apartment in East L.A. There I was, driving around in my Mercedes with two babies in the back seat, in a completely Mexican neighborhood where I couldn't understand anyone and they couldn't understand me. God bless that nanny and her neighbors, they embraced me and helped me, but it wasn't a place I could live long-term. I was having terrible panic attacks. I didn't know where to go or what to do. I called my dad and told him I was at the end of my rope.

I had been planning to go back home to Minnesota for a visit in a few weeks so my parents could meet the new baby. My husband had a grand total of $10,000 in the bank. Ten thousand dollars—what we used to spend on a weekend trip. What I used to make in a night as a call girl! I took half the money, $5000— which I felt I was more than owed—and changed our tickets to leave early. I fled back to my parents' small house in Minnesota and tried to figure out what to do. Two kids under the age of three, no job, an estranged husband and no money. Things didn't look good.

My parents were wonderful, but after several months they said, "You need to get a job and an apartment, and figure out what to do with the rest of your life." I had my whole life in storage in LA. My parents started really getting on my back; my husband was calling me all the time, trying to get me to come home; I finally told my parents that I was returning to LA.

Back in Business

I really thought I had left being a call girl behind when I got married. I loved my husband, though he turned out to be a real jerk. Our reconciliation didn't last long, of course, and we eventually divorced. Very soon I was a single woman with two children my husband refused to help support. He claimed he didn't have any money, and he was probably right. I didn't want to chase him down and drag him through the courts if he didn't want to support his own kids—I just wanted to move on.

But I realized things had really changed in the five or so years I was out of the business. There weren't any jobs out there anymore where I'd command four or five thousand dollars for one night. I looked around and saw that there were really no big madams in Los Angeles anymore. There was no Madam Alex, there was no Heidi Fleiss; Rose and Sophia had gotten busted and fled back to Mexico; the glory days were over.

I called my friend Candy, and she gave me $2000. On the condition that I pay her back, of course. I never did. I felt like I had done more than enough for her. When I first met her, Candy was very unhappily married, looking to leave her husband, but had no way of supporting herself. I liked her; she was a sweet girl and I wanted to help her. I didn't have any money to give her, but I set her up with the girl who arranged the trip to Brunei. She made quite a splash with the Sultan's brother. Her money problems were over, to say the least. I figured she owed me; that $2000 was the least she could do.

I was in a really desperate place. I had no money, bills to pay, two kids and no prospects of any income anytime soon. I needed cash, badly. So I placed another ad in *LA Express*. Same thing: *Hot Massage/Hot Girl* with my cell phone number. I got a few calls one night and took one because it was close by. It was from a guy staying at Le Mondrian Hotel, a very trendy place to be at that time. He gave me his room number and told me to come right over.

A fairly young guy in his early thirties, nice-looking, answered the door. His face was vaguely familiar; I couldn't figure out who he was but I knew I had seen him somewhere before. I shrugged it off and we started partying. We did a lot of drinking; he was doing a lot of freebasing (smoking cocaine). We tried to fool around; I did my best, but the drugs were catching up to him and he was unable to achieve penetration. Just too wasted. So he asked me to call someone else, another guy, and bring him to the party. He could at least watch us fool around. I called a male friend of mine who was happy to come over and join us. The three of us continued to drink heavily, and we all fooled around a little bit. Our client continued to freebase. He couldn't get enough. He had very dark circles under his eyes and looked like he had been up for days. The way he was hitting that pipe, I was sure he had been.

Our client enjoyed talking about all kinds of way-out-there sex fantasies all through the night. He was a big talker; we got a big three-way discussion going about all kinds of outrageous sex acts. My friend Tommy and I were coming up with all kinds of wild stories to keep him happy. He kept telling us, "This is how I relax."

We moved on to the show—me having sex with Tommy as our client sat in a chair freebasing and watching us. Tommy swings both ways, so he was happy to oblige. Specifically, our client wanted to watch me give Tommy a blowjob. So I did. As we rolled around on the floor, my friend whispered in my ear, "You know who this is, right? Matt LeBlanc from *Friends*?" Oh yeah, right!

Matt was actually a really nice guy, obviously very intelligent. He didn't want us to leave, even at 4 in the morning. Tommy liked him too, the two of them were having a great conversation, all three of us were walking around naked for hours, partying. There were quite a lot of drugs there. Tommy and I snorted some blow, but neither of us were freebasers. We were all very high, no doubt about it. At one point Matt tried to get me to bring another girl over, and I made a bunch of calls, but couldn't find anyone. The whole night was very long and hazy.

Matt paid both me and Tommy before we left—we were partying so hard I can't even remember how much—it was $500 each, or maybe a thousand each. He was pleasant, polite, a cool guy. Honestly, I think it was just that he wanted some company, some people to party with, and that's why he called an ad out of the paper. It wasn't so much about having sex with somebody; I think he mainly wanted some non-judgmental company. Really, he was more of a voyeur than anything else. Besides wanting to watch me and Tommy perform sex acts together, he was happy just to hang out with us all night. I'm sure this wasn't the kind of night he could share with his other "Friends."

Look, just because someone is an actor on TV doesn't mean they don't have problems or needs. He was simply taking care of his. This was hardly the kind of partying he could do with his real friends. He had no image to keep up in front of us. Freebasing, watching other people get it on…no, I couldn't imagine him doing that with Jennifer Aniston or Courteney Cox.

When I got home that night, it almost seemed like I made it up. For months after that, every time I turned on the TV and saw an ad for *Friends*, I would jump a little and turn the channel. I couldn't believe it.

It's Not the Nineties Anymore

For several years old friends sent me clients, nobody famous, and certainly not for the same money I used to get. It's not the nineties anymore, that's for sure. But once this business has gotten into your system, it stays a part of you. Where else are you going to get a thousand dollars cash for an hour of your time?

Well, the truth is you're not anymore. I was in the business in its heyday—back when Madam Alex and Heidi ruled the town. Good-looking men, rich famous guys, who ordered Cristal champagne for me in their suites at the best hotels in the world and paid me thousands of dollars besides. That's the kind of business I was used to. Plenty of girls got sent on those types of jobs back then. Nowadays, there aren't any jobs or madams like that. Everyone's in business for themselves, on the internet. Selling themselves online for maybe $200 or $300. That's crazy.

The whole newspaper ad thing is over too. I'm sure famous guys are still using the ads, but it's all online now. LA Exotics.com is the perfect example. The girls are just so young and beautiful…unbelievable. This is LA, after all, where so many girls are flawless. They're young, their bodies are perfect, their faces are gorgeous. It's like ordering something on Amazon.com...customers rate their services with one to five stars!

Those newspaper ads that used to be so popular—lots of them with a tiny postage-stamp-size black and white picture—that all seemed harmless. I would never put my picture out over the internet. But that's where all the action is now. No madams, no newspapers. Everything is online these days. There are plenty of girls making money selling themselves through the internet.

And oh, what I want to tell those girls. If I could grab them all and make them listen, this is what I'd tell them: Go to school and get a degree, and at the very least learn some solid, marketable skills. Go to beauty school and become an esthetician; or nursing school and get a CNA degree—because the party will end. Don't think of this as a never-ending stream of income, and—impossible to tell young girls, I know—don't think you'll be 23 years old forever. The problem is that very soon there will be younger, prettier, wilder girls in the game too. It's all going to come to an end, and you'd better have some way of earning a living.

The Ironies of Life

Four years ago this woman madam had a hookup with a bunch of Arabs in town. She was kind of like Madam Alex used to be. One of the princes from Saudi Arabia came into town, and I saw him. He owned a bunch of horses, had a winner in the Kentucky Derby, was a big player at the racetrack in Del Mar. He adored me from the minute I showed up at his hotel. We took a limo ride to his estate in Monrovia, and I was the first one to be with him. He liked to smoke weed, so we had brought some with us. He had a brought a musical group with him, who were on their way to a date at Radio City Music Hall. And this prince paid them fifty grand to stop at his place in Monrovia and play at our little private party! This Arab music was unbelievable; they were like the U2 of the Middle East. Our host was a gentleman; everything was wonderful, we had a great time. It reminded me of the old days.

I saw this Prince one more time, then I read in the newspaper that he had died of a heart attack. I freaked out; I couldn't believe it. Much later, I found out from another friend of mine that he actually died from complications of liposuction. He was the last big paying client I ever really had.

But I was ready to get out of the business for real by that time. Like I say, it sure wasn't what it used to be, and I didn't want to be doing that kind of work while bringing up two kids on my own. I've never gotten a dime in child support, and it's tough, but I got out of the business and stayed out. The fact is that I'm on government aid—$700 a month. People would be amazed if they knew how many people in Santa Monica are actually on government aid. If the county knew how much my apartment really rented for—which is $2500 a month—my son, daughter and I would be packed off to Compton, immediately. Fortunately, my landlord helps me out—he tells the county workers that I pay $600 a month for my place because it's a rent-controlled building. In return for the $600 rent, I help him manage the building. This way we live in a nice neighborhood and the kids attend an excellent public school. The Lord works in mysterious ways.

I have been increasingly drawn to religion as I get older, and have become a devout Catholic. I was brought up that way, but really slid away from the Church for many years. Now I find my faith very comforting and a real source of strength. My kids and I go to church every Sunday. And here's the funniest thing. Arnold Schwarzenegger, who is now the Governor of California, also attends my church. I see him, Maria, all their kids and the Secret Service detail all the time! Last Easter we were standing at the door together after the Easter service and Arnold smiled at me and said, "Beautiful service, wasn't it?" All I could do was smile and nod. He doesn't remember me, of course—he thinks I'm the nice lady who teaches Sunday School. I have to laugh to myself when I think about it.

As of this date it's been four years since I've had sex of any kind. I now live a completely celibate life. For the past few years I have not felt very sexy. Of course I'm older now, I don't know if it's hormonal, or just because I'm a stressed-out overwhelmed single mom. I've got a lot on my plate. My son and daughter are great kids, but by the end of each day—cooking, cleaning, homework, after-school activities, friends, you name it, I am just completely mentally exhausted.

I certainly went from one extreme to the other—having sex all the time and making tons of money doing it to not having sex at all and having no money. Life is funny. I was talking to a friend of mine the other day, and she said, "You're still a beautiful woman, you're in the prime of your life, you should be having the best sex of your life!" I just laughed, but my friend persisted. "I mean it, you're wasting your life. This is the time you should be feeling your sexiest. Pretty soon you're not going to have that option anymore."

I went to college. I never thought of being a call girl as all I could be. But then I got married and had children and thought that was going to be the rest of my life. Now I'm nearing 40 years old, a single mom, on welfare, and some days I worry. I wonder every day, *What am I going to do?* I can't live off county aid for the rest of my life—it ends in a year no matter what. The government only provides aid for five years, except under very special circumstances. I mean, if everyone here in California lived off county aid all their lives, there'd be no money left at all in the budget. The idea is to help people get on their feet, get a job, and eventually not live off the government.

So, I do the best I can. I have jewelry parties at night some-times, I sell cosmetics to my friends. I've even been in touch with my modeling agency again lately—they're talking about finding some work for me in their Classic Woman division. Ever since *Desperate Housewives* became a hit 40-something women are hot again, and they're looking to capitalize on that trend. Of course, I need to get some work done on my teeth before that will happen, which will cost thousands of dollars I don't have.

I want to be someone, a professional person, but I can't quite figure out how to do it. After-school care is so expensive. I want to keep my kids in the Santa Monica school district, of course—the public schools outside the area are horrible. I cringe all the time now that I have my own girl, who is growing up fast. A beautiful girl who lives within walking distance of the Third Street Promenade. Where else are my kids going to want to hang out when they get into high school? When they're 16 or 17 and want to go places with their friends? There is so much going on in LA that is underground, and I'm very afraid for my girl, particularly. The dangers of living here are always on my mind as I watch her mature.

It's hard sometimes, but I'm not disappointed with my life. Why should I live in regret? Accept your choices, laugh and live. I'm doing OK. If I had been better prepared to live on my own, if I had gone to college, if I had seriously pursued acting or any other career—if I had done any of these things, would it have deterred me from sleeping with men for money? I don't know. A lot of ifs. All I know is this is my life and this is where I ended up.

And here's the bottom line: If I had a chance to sleep with someone for $1500 tonight I would do it. That's just the truth. I wouldn't go for $200 or $300, but a nice businessman, a pleasant dinner and $1500? You bet I would go. I used to do it for the thrill—now I would do it for the money. I'm not going to be all prissy and judgmental and say, "Oh, I would never do anything like that again."

Does sleeping with men for money mean that I have no morals, or that I don't like myself? I don't believe it does. I have enough self-esteem and feel that I'm enough of a whole person to know that sleeping with men for money—at least in my case—had nothing to do with low self-esteem. Call me a realist. Men need or want certain things that they can't always get from a wife or girlfriend, and what is wrong with providing it?

Everything is going to be fine. I trust in God.

Carly Milne

Photograph by: Todd Williamson

Carly Milne

Porn and Hollywood

I got in like most girls do—by answering an ad. I became an adult industry publicist in 2002. For those of you that don't live your lives in a media wind tunnel, a publicist represents a client to the media, getting them coverage in newspapers, magazines and websites across the world, which theoretically raises their profile. My foray into the world of adult entertainment—or porn, if you're not squeamish about the word—happened both on purpose and by accident. Though I was a consumer—my boyfriend and I occasionally rented adult films and had purchased a few toys—it was a world I knew very little about. Of course I knew who Jenna Jameson was, but who didn't? There was something about working in the trenches of the business that both intrigued and terrified me. My job hunt led me to debating between a gig with E! and the porn job, and porn won out, as I wanted to write a book about what it was like on the inside.

Publicity is complicated. Many people think it's just about writing press releases and sending them out, then waiting for a response—but no. It's constant calling and follow-ups, sometimes to the point of annoyance. It's taking people out to lunch, remembering birthdays and holidays, and maintaining relationships so your clients are handled favorably. It's pitching your heart out to the point of exhaustion. It's driving clients from interview to interview, briefing them on what the subject matter is and—at times—coaching them on their response. It's trying to figure out creative ways to include your clients in topics the press are covering that don't directly include them. It's shipping product all over the globe. It's assembling bios and press kits and accompanying websites. It's traveling to do press tours. It's nerve-wracking. And you're always trying to prove yourself to everyone involved.

But it goes even deeper than that. On one hand you have a client who doesn't really understand why they would need publicity and how it all works, but they hire a publicist because their competitors have one and their sales are higher, so they deduce that a publicist must be what's missing from their winning formula. So you accept the gig and get treated like dirt for a while because really, you're just a sap of expenses... that is, until you land them their first big press hit and they consistently see their name on heavily-trafficked websites. On the other hand you have the press who oftentimes need everything yesterday—interviews, pictures, set visits... you name it, they're on deadline for it. Soon the client is never happy with what you get them—they always want more, it's never enough. And on the odd occasion when you have to deny the press, they sometimes get angrily feisty and threatening. Thus, it becomes a delicate balancing act of trying to appease both sides—and to an extent, babysitting—while attempting to keep your sanity in check. And when everything goes wrong, it always winds up being your fault, whether it's really your fault or not.

So yes, I expected mayhem and debauchery mixed with professionalism and normalcy, and when I became a porn publicist, I saw all of that and more. But what I didn't expect was how much adult and mainstream entertainment were intertwined. To say I didn't see a connection would be not only naive, but an outright lie—rock stars and porn stars go together like chocolate and peanut butter, after all. But what I didn't expect was how interconnected their worlds were, how many secret relationships of varying types were forged, and how uneasy both sides appeared to be about the whole thing.

Hal Sparks and the Congressmen

Admittedly, I didn't know the first thing about promoting a porn starlet. What I soon learned was that porn starlets came in all sorts of different packages. There were those who were educated and held down several jobs before turning to the smut business, there were those who dropped out of high school and never worked a real day in their lives, and for as many that have handled some kind of abuse issue in their past, there were an equal number that were in the business simply because they love to fuck, love to watch people fuck, and love people to watch them fuck. But regardless of the variety to choose from, I was constantly warned of one thing from business owners, directors and fellow publicists: I did not want to promote them.

"Sure I do," I would argue. "I mean, if they want to be promoted, why wouldn't I want to work with them?"

"It's not like that," they'd tell me. "They *want* you to promote them. They want you to make them the next Jenna Jameson and Julia Roberts all rolled up into one. If you attempt to help them with that goal, they will make your life hell. Bet on it. They always seem normal at first, but they all have a Trojan horse."

Ahh, the Trojan horse. I'd heard many a story about this starlet melting down on set or that starlet denouncing her time as a porn star as she ran from it, only to launch a triumphant comeback a few months later. I didn't doubt that the industry was hard on the girls who chose to perform on camera. With porn being so image-based, they were under a tremendous amount of pressure from all sides to conform to a certain ideal. The only problem was that ideal was different from person to person. While the industry wanted them to be wanton sex goddesses at every given moment, society and the mainstream media wanted them to be more closeted about their sexuality under certain circumstances, and less so in others. Some of the top names in the industry—such as the Jenna Jamesons, Nina Hartleys and Tera Patricks of the world—figured out how to walk the tightrope expertly. The rest wind up with a pseudo case of multiple personality disorder that acted up at the most inopportune times.

When I decided to take a full-time job with a leading adult video distribution company, I sat down with the owners and let them fill me in on all their properties and the girls associated with said properties. I was told that these girls were under contract, and as such, they were happy to be there and wanted to become stars. The main girls to focus on, they told me, were two contract girls with gonzo director and reality-show sweetheart Seymore Butts and three that were signed to high-end feature director Michael Ninn's company, Ninn Worx. But both of the owners—who I took to calling Boss 1 and Boss 2— had a particular liking for one of the Ninn Worx girls, a leggy, 20-year-old looker named Anais.

"She's a really good kid," Boss 2 told me. "She could easily become the face of this company, and we really think she'll be huge with the right person behind her. She's a little quiet and needs to break out of her shell, but she's got a lot more promise than any of those other whooeres." He punctuated his comment by sweeping his arm in the direction of a poster on the wall that depicted all the Ninn Worx contract stars. He always called the girls "whooers" rather than just "whores," as if it meant they were worse than your garden-variety hookers.

"What's the deal with the others?" I asked.

"Well, Georgia's sweet but she's never here. She doesn't live in town, so I'm not sure we're going to extend her contract," he told me. "Wanda is out of the country, Nikita isn't in the business anymore, and Angel is a fucking piece of work."

I laughed. "How do you mean?"

"Well, she's just a total whooer. I mean, more than the rest of them are. Last year during the Adult Entertainment Expo she upgraded her room at the Venetian Hotel by giving free blowjobs to the front desk staff."

Fucking on camera for money, acceptable. Fucking off camera for goods and or services, not acceptable, I thought, making a mental note in my head. It was endlessly interesting to me that the girls fucking on film was one thing, but if they fucked anywhere else it was entirely another. Not to mention, there were plenty of company owners who understood the importance of having these women represent their company, especially when it came time for the Adult Entertainment Expo. They were tramps, whores and useless trash...with the exception of when they were helping turn a profit for a manufacturer and distributor.

Regardless of what Boss 2 had said, I endeavored to meet each of the five girls to get an idea of what their goals were. Georgia Adair was happy with anything and was ready for whatever. She preferred to live outside of Los Angeles, yet somehow got into the industry courtesy of an online modeling and chat site she and her husband ran as their business. She was the typical starlet in the sense that she had blonde hair and big boobs, but she also didn't think she deserved to be famous just because she was on-camera, which was a refreshing change. Angel Cassidy wanted to charge the world for everything, discussing plans for a new feature on her website where her fans could pay for the right to worship her (or something to that effect...she already sold them her used underwear and sex toys, so she didn't think this was in any way unreasonable.) I never really got a straight answer from her about how she got into the business, but near as I could tell she also went the online sex site route, decided to do modeling for adult magazines, then segued into film and video, sometimes with her boyfriend. She definitely had the entitlement thing going on, but by the same token was happy to have any mention of herself in the press no matter how tiny. Mari Possa, a Seymore Butts girl (not to mention his then-girl-friend), wanted to capitalize on the notoriety she had from doing his reality show, *Family Business* on Showtime, and start doing more interviews and layouts despite some underlying shyness. Her story was a little more unusual, having started out as Seymore's assistant, becoming his girlfriend, then deciding to make the jump into porn star, much to her parents' chagrin. Flower Tucci, also with Seymore Butts, wanted the same as Mari did except she didn't have an issue with shyness. In fact, she was willing to show her bountiful ass at the slightest provocation. It was almost shocking to find out she was a mother. I never did find out how she began her career. And then I met Anais.

It happened on a Monday morning. In some ways I'm a creature of habit. As soon as I'd get into the office I liked to shut the door, light my candles and incense, and start my morning surfing the gossip and news sites to see who's posted what about any of the people I work with, be it rumor and conjecture or a press release I've sent out. Once I got that out of the way I'd be ready to face the day. There was something about having a little silence while easing myself into the porno ambiance, so surfing the gossip sites was the most inoffensive way to do this. That morning, however, I hit the ground running. I walked up to the office and greeted porn world's manager to the stars Lucky, who had brought Anais with him to meet with me for the first time and do an interview for *Oui* magazine. I'd locked down the cover for her based on her photos. Now I just had to give them the text to back it up.

In her photos, Anais looked ethereal and almost unreal. She was slender but toned with perfect 36-Cs (thanks to plastic surgeon to the stars Garth Fisher, responsible for the breasts of practically everyone and supposedly the man who single-handedly constructed Brook Burke), greenish blue eyes and long, naturally blonde hair. But she wasn't the stereotypical bleached out inflated porn star. Rather, she had more of a high fashion quality. Her pictures conveyed an old-soul attitude that belied her true age. She may have only been 20, but her photos made her look much more worldly and sophisticated than the freshly-scrubbed kid who walked into my office. Decked out in jeans and a wife beater with not a stitch of make-up on her face, Anais looked more like she was 16 and waiting to be asked to the prom rather than a sex goddess who gets drilled by some of the top swordsmen in the industry.

Both she and Lucky took a seat and we chatted for a while. I wanted to get a feel for who she was and what she wanted to do with her life, just like I had with all the other girls. Anais was well spoken and didn't mince words, which I found refreshing. When something was on her mind, she just said it. I could tell that she wasn't completely being herself with me, but I suspected that was mostly because we'd never met before. I did my best to make her comfortable.

Lucky excused himself so Anais and I could answer the questions for the magazine. She proved to be a smart and spunky chick with a take-no-prisoners attitude about her life, and I admired the aplomb with which she answered the most intimate of questions for the *Oui* interview. But in my delicate morning state, having not executed my start-of-the-day easing into triple-X, there was something jarring about sitting behind my desk typing like mad in a desperate attempt to record everything that's being said while this 20 year-old stunner sits across from me explaining how she thinks the sloppier the blow job the better, and when she's done giving a guy head there's usually a puddle of drool at his feet, and how she's so dominant...all before 9:30am.

With the interview out of the way, I talked to Lucky about whether or not he'd like tickets to the Free Speech Coalition's fundraiser, Night of the Stars. He took two tickets and decided he would bring Anais with him. That Saturday members of the FSC and the industry gathered to dine on pre-fab meals and watered-down cocktails. Everyone gathered out front of the Sheraton Universal to mingle and chat while a minstrel wandered the crowd. It was always interesting to attend these events, with the adult performers in their best evening wear—some of whom chose stripper-wear as their attire—mingling with members of Congress. The members of the industry were always comfortable. The members of Congress? Not so much. It wasn't so much that they were there under duress as much as they appeared worried the industry members would break out into some kind of sexual activity at any moment—as if grown adults who fucked for a living couldn't keep it in their evening wear for a few hours.

I arrived with my yoga teacher and Seymore's assistant, then met up with Seymore, Flower, Mari and Cousin Stevie— Seymore Butts' cousin and a major player on the show *Family Business*. Shortly afterward Lucky showed up with Anais in tow, looking even more demure than she had earlier that week in my office. To be honest, it kind of creeped me out. I wondered if this girl was really meant to be in the porn industry. I wondered if any of them were, really, and even if I should be promoting them at all.

As I was mentally debating this, Seymore's assistant said, "Look, isn't that Hal Sparks?"

And lo, walking through the crowd with a purple faux-hawk was Hal Sparks, he of *Queer As Folk* and *I Love The 80s, 70s...* and just about any other VH1 show that had humorous talking heads. Naturally, Stevie wanted his picture taken with Hal, so we all steered our asses over in his general direction and started chatting him up. I was granted permission to take pictures. Then Seymore joined us, seeing as he and Hal shared a network. As he was saying his hellos to everyone Anais looked Seymore up and down and announced, "You look like a pimp."

The most amusing thing about the whole evening was when the politicos started loosening up, or not, in the case of the assemblyman who was seated—rather uncomfortably—at my company's table. Another kept insisting on taking pictures of my yoga teacher, who finally snapped at him that she wasn't a porn star. He didn't see the big deal and demanded to know why she wouldn't allow him to take pictures of her because "I'm not going to publish them anywhere."

Hal wandered by our table again and chatted up a few people, spending a little more time with Anais than anyone else. It was refreshing that he didn't seem to give a shit whether someone was in porn or not. Most of the industry liked to grouse that mainstream stars looked down their noses at them unless they could be used for something, but Hal certainly wasn't behaving in this manner. Later Seymore's assistant pulled me aside and told me Hal had asked for Anais' number.

"Really?"

"Yes, that's what Anais told me."

"Did she give it to him?"

"I don't know."

I laughed. I had a contact at Page Six that would love that little tidbit. But first, I wanted to make sure it was okay with Anais before I ran with it. The problem was, I wasn't getting the feeling that she wanted to be promoted as much as my bosses wanted to promote her. All the other girls—Georgia, Angel, Mari and Flower—were already acting as if I were their best friend. Anais was a harder sell. Hmm. What could I do to get her to open up to me the same way the others did?

I had a plan: a trip to Disneyland.

Now, understandably this whole game plan sounded incredibly creepy, and if I were a male publicist there's no doubt in my mind that many would suspect an ulterior motive. My intent was nothing of the sort. To my mind, if my bosses felt that Anais was the great, white hope in terms of promoting the company, I wanted to do what made them happy. There was no question that she was a very pretty girl. The question was, did she really want to be in porn? Because if she didn't want to be there, I didn't want to push her. Based on what I'd seen she still had some very childlike qualities about her. So what better place to discuss it than the neutral territory of the happiest place on earth?

The following Monday I sat down with my bosses and pitched them the idea. They thought I was on crack, but agreed that there might be some method to my madness. Reluctantly, they agreed to let me take a day out of the office to take a porn star to Disneyland. And on the company dime! I called Anais to ask her if she'd like to go.

"Are you kidding me?"

"Nope."

"How did you get Boss 2 to agree to that? He's cheap!"

"Don't worry about that," I laughed. "If you want to go, the offer is open."

"Yeah, I wanna go!"

We made arrangements for me to pick her up on set the night before so she could spend the night at my apartment—she didn't drive, and actually lived about three hours outside of L.A. —and then we'd leave first thing in the morning.

I discussed my plan with a friend in the industry who was a retired star. She'd worked on set with Ninn many times and knew all the girls, so I wanted to get her opinion on my game plan with Anais.

"I think it's a great way to break the ice," she said. "But be careful—I wouldn't let that little girl act fool you too much."

"Oh?" I asked, my ears perking up. I'd had so many people assure me that Anais was really truly not like the other girls that any mention of a Trojan horse was cause for alarm.

"Yeah, you know she escorts, right?"

"What!?"

"Oh yeah. People on set say she makes quite a living off hooking."

I quickly processed what she'd said. The innocent young girl I was taking to Disneyland was a hooker? Nah. Couldn't be. "I don't know about that," I said. "Are you sure he's got the right girl? It's not Angel?"

"Oh, she does it too," she told me. "But it was definitely clear— they said Anais did it."

It wasn't at all shocking to me that a porn star would hook. After all, many of the girls in the industry would actually use their star power to command exorbitantly high rates with high-rollers and A-listers willing to pay for airfare, hotel and up to six figures with some of porn's top names. Hell, some even claimed to know for a fact that supermodels like Naomi Campbell were for hire at a high-five figure price tag for one night. But most of the girls were tight lipped about it. Some of the agencies were online and would feature pictures of their girls for hire. Nine times out of ten a girl would cry foul and claim a company was full of shit for posting their information. One time out of ten it would actually be bullshit. Though most are quiet about extra-curricular activities because of the IRS, some don't talk about it because, ironically, sometimes there's a stigma attached to girls who decide to hook for extra income. I didn't doubt that a lot of porn girls hooked, because they could make some good money off of it. I doubted Anais hooked because this was a girl who didn't seem to want to be fucking for a living, period.

Regardless, I met Anais on set. She wrapped around 1am, at which point we hopped in the car and drove home, chattering away about anything and everything. The coolness I had felt before was gone as we talked about our upbringings, our favorite foods, and how we found ourselves in the world of porn. Seeing as we'd been hitting it off so well I decided to broach the hooking subject, albeit not directly.

"So I'm curious," I started. "You know other girls in the industry who hook, right?"

"Oh yeah," she nodded. "Wanda does it. She makes a lot of money, too."

"What do you think about that?"

"I could never do it," she said, shaking her head firmly. "It's just not my thing. I mean, more power to the girls that do, but for me it's just...I couldn't do it. In porn I get to know the people I work with and I get to choose who I work with, you know? There's something about hooking that's just not my thing. Never."

She seemed sincere enough, so I let it go. I decided to ask her more about her background, and was surprised to find she was a mother at her young age. Not only that, but she had been married. Her ex-husband was abusive and she wound up leaving him, and not long after she got involved in porn. Her introduction to the industry was easy—her cousin was a star by the name of Crystal Summers and helped facilitate the move. Long before she was a part of the industry, Anais was joining Crystal at parties in the Playboy Mansion, fielding offers from rich celebrities and businessmen to have her as their kept woman. According to her, she fended off their advances and made the decision to do porn at 18 after she'd spent some time with Crystal on a set and met Lucky, her now agent and manager.

After a pit-stop for some Ben n' Jerry's (she wanted some to celebrate the end of filming), we crashed out for the night in preparation of the day ahead. And after roughly four hours of sleep we got up and hopped back in the car, each of us carrying stuffed animal backpacks (it's a must to behave like a child when you're going to Disneyland), and rolled into the parking lot just in time to catch some breakfast before jumping on some rides.

The day was a blur. We rode rides, we ate lots of stuff that was bad for us, we ran around like crazed children and giggled uncontrollably at the most ridiculous things. We took pictures with the characters and paid silly amounts of money for shots of us screaming on Tower of Terror, for which we bought matching frames. And then somewhere between the Haunted Mansion and Splash Mountain, she brought up the business.

"You know, nobody's really done anything with me PR-wise," she said. "I mean, the publicist before you got me into *Flaunt* magazine and I did some dancing for Carmen Electra and Dave Navarro's bachelor party that aired on MTV, but other than that? Nothing. And it sucks."

I was almost stunned to hear her say it, partially because I was having such a good time that I forgot that this was part of the reason why we went to the park in the first place. "So what are you saying?" I asked.

"I'm saying that I have a limited amount of time in the industry, and if I'm going to make the most of it financially, I've gotta build a name for myself. Like Jenna Jameson."

I smiled. "So are you saying you're ready for me to push? Because if you're saying you are, I'm going to go for it."

She nodded. "I'm ready."

I went back to the office the next day and told The Bosses what she'd said. They were pleased.

From there I jumped into action. If the mainstream media was going to accept her as part of this new, take-charge generation of women in porn I had to make sure that she was positioned correctly. Television media like the 20/20s of the world were only interested in seeing the victim that they could exploit to make the industry look like the terrible place most of America was comfortable believing it was. But the *Maxims* and the like? Not their style. I knew that the best way to position Anais was to present her as a smart but gorgeous newcomer that chose to be in that world with no regrets—no victim, she. I ran it past her and she was enthusiastic about the plan, noting that she didn't feel that what she was doing was something to be ashamed of, and it was myth she was more than willing to help demystify. I started teasing media contacts with pictures and little tidbits of information on her.

Within days I got called with an opportunity to book her as eye candy for a photo shoot appearing in a foreign edition of *Vanity Fair*. The Page Six item on her and Hal Sparks ran (though I eventually found out it was all bullshit, but more on that later.) *Stuff* magazine reviewed her title film and ran a picture of the box cover with the review. I started working on getting her a gig as a spokesmodel for a high-end fashion line. People were calling me to get quotes from her for their articles. I wrote about her and posted her pictures with tons of websites. Adult media started harassing me to meet her. The reaction was getting a little overwhelming, even for me.

On one occasion one of the press members asked me to bring her by to hang out, even though he'd already met her before. I asked her to go with me, but she bristled, wanting to wait in the car. When I went inside one of my press contacts there told me the *New York Times* was doing a piece on women in adult entertainment and made a passive-aggressive mention that it was too bad Anais hadn't come with me, because she might've been able to get interviewed for the piece. I told her when I got back to the car.

"So what? I don't care," she said bitterly. "Let Jenna Jameson do it."

I should've taken that as a big-ass hint, but I didn't. I reasoned that perhaps she felt like she was being trotted out like a whore—or whooer, as Boss 2 had called them—and the last thing I wanted to do was make her feel like that. So I let it go.

Britney Spears and Tommy Lee

I called up a fellow publicist to tell her about my issues, but she had her own issues to deal with, however. Her charge was a contract star named Jesse Jane, a fresh-faced Texan who started her porn career by approaching the head of the company with the desire to be his next contract star. At the time she was a Hawaiian Tropics model, but had counted a stint as a Hooters waitress among her pre-porn careers. It turned out that Jesse had taken to hanging out with Britney Spears' manager... and after a weekend in the Hamptons with a group of people including Ms. Spears, it seemed she had made an enemy out of Kevin Federline.

"What happened?" I asked over lunch one day.

"Apparently Jesse went out to party in the Hamptons, and Britney was, like, totally into her," she explained. "I guess they were all touchy feely and flirty to the point where Kevin got super jealous, packed up all their shit and flew them out to Florida a week earlier than they planned."

"Seriously?"

She shrugged. "Who knows, dude. Jesse is a porn star, and it's not like Britney is going to admit to any of this."

I made a mental note to ask Jesse about it the next time I saw her, and thankfully, I didn't have to wait too long. I took a trip to New York to take Cousin Stevie on a press tour, making the rounds at *Penthouse, Maxim* and the like with the Showtime cameras trailing his every move. It just so happened that Jesse Jane was also in town preparing to go on the Howard Stern show for the first time. After meeting her and her publicist for dinner and hitting Hiro for a night of dancing (during which she was approached by some frat boy type who said, "Has anyone ever told you that you look like Jesse Jane?"), the three of us retired to her hotel room to snack on dried fruit and nuts and talk sex advice. Sure, she was seeing Tommy Lee at the time. But more importantly, what was the deal with her and Britney?

"She's hot," Jesse said, smiling widely. "I'm telling you, there's no way that girl hasn't been with other girls."

"So was Kevin Federline really jealous of you two?"

She rolled her eyes. "Ugh, he is such a wigger. I have no idea why she's with him. But yeah, any time she and I would start talking, he'd show up and take her away somewhere until he made them leave the Hamptons."

"That sucks," I told her, then listened to tales of how she's hung out with most of the guys from N'Sync and how funny and nice they were. This gave me pause for thought. "Do you think any of that relationship with K-Fed has to do with getting over Justin?"

Jesse nodded. "Here's the thing about her and Justin—he cheated on her all the time, but the difference was that he cheated on her with people who weren't directly related to them. The reason why they broke up is because Britney decided to go for it too, but she went for it with that choreographer guy, Wade."

I changed the subject. "So how's Tommy Lee in bed?"

"Ohmigod, he's the best," she swooned. "I've never had someone like him before. I mean, one minute he can be pounding the hell out of you, and the next he's holding you super close and staring into your eyes and being so tender... it's a trip, man. It's a rollercoaster with him."

Apparently it wasn't a roller coaster that was meant to last, though, as Jesse stopped seeing him not long after, and started seeing Kid Rock, much to her publicist's chagrin. "I know she wants to be like Pam Anderson, but does she have to do it like this?" she moaned to me one afternoon over lunch. I sort of sympathized with her plight, but I was too intrigued by the hook-ups to look at it as a tragedy.

The Comedian, Charlie Sheen and Michael Keaton

I started hearing tales all over the place—Stormy Daniels told me about Vince Neil's childish behavior (they saw each other back when she was a stripper), and someone told me a great story about Julie Knight hooking up with Carrot Top (if I remember correctly, she tied him up and spanked him in Vegas one night). Seeing as I was working with Nina Hartley on a book project, I called her up, curious to see if she'd had any interesting hook-ups over the years. Nina had started her career as a stripper and branched out into nude modeling, videos, and even mainstream performances—most notably in *Boogie Nights*—over her 20-year career. Surely the legend of the industry had something to share.

"I'm not a celeb chaser, but I do know I have plenty of fans in straight Hollywood," she told me. "I've heard through second and third parties, everyone likes porn, why would Hollywood be different?"

"Well, I doubted it was, really—I've had enough run-ins with people there to know that. But come on…you've got to have at least one good story to tell."

"Okay, I've got one I can tell you," she relented. "I was dancing in Pennsylvania, and I knew this comic—he was very tall and did a couple of TV things in the early 90s. I wasn't into picking people up on the road, but I figured he wasn't going to kill me considering he was famous, so I arranged for him to come and visit me after work. In 15 years of feature dancing I'd had maybe five guests total, but I was titillated by stranger sex and getting some on the road, so I went for it. Not because he was famous, but I felt safe because he was.

"Anyway. He's gotta be 6'5. We talked for a while, and of course, he was funny. Now, I'm not a size queen, so when he got naked and I looked at him, I thought, 'Thank God he looks normal.' What I didn't take into account that he looked normal for his size, but if he were 5'6 his penis would've been huge—he was well over eight inches! He was *big* big—much bigger than me, so the only position that worked was with me on my stomach. It was the only time we ever did it. We've run into each other since then and I know he's never forgotten, but he hasn't pursued it with me."

She went on to tell me stories of the Emmy-award winning actor who was in LAX, having just gotten off the plane from his honeymoon, and actually walked backwards to see if it was really her walking through the terminal, as well as her hook-up with a famous rap star. But what she found most interesting is not only why Hollywood types were interested in sleeping with her, but how agents and managers stood in their way most of the time.

"Lots of mucky-mucks in Hollywood would like to have fun with someone like me, but agents say don't go there," she told me. "What they don't know is I'm not going to go to the tabloids and talk or name names—that's not why I do this. Back in the late 80s there were lots of porn actress and Hollywood star hook ups—Ginger Lynn and Charlie Sheen, Penny Morgan and the guy who played an older doctor character on a sitcom set in Florida, Jeanna Fine and Michael Keaton...all of those got blown up in the tabloids, and I'm just not a kiss and tell person like that. But I'm curious, and it turns out they're just like you and me. A couple of them have been good—they've got some moves! The big tall one was arrogant so he had no issues—and some of them are like a clumsy person just like any other, but I find it sweet because with me, most have seen me on camera...but they're looking for validation as sexual humans. Nobody has ever asked how they were, but I can tell that's the subtext because I'm a professional."

The Hollywood Studio Execs

Meanwhile, I also worked on the other girls. I landed Mari an interview and layout with Florida-based adult magazine and went to work on getting her more exposure and photo shoots with other photographers, I followed up Anais' *Oui* cover with Angel, and I started working with Georgia on her schedule and when she was in town so she could do some media interviews. Flower and I plotted some work, but nothing could really be done until she had some photos done, which she was waiting on a photographer friend for. She had recently lost weight and wanted to show off her new body. I could empathize, so I told her to let me know when she was ready.

It was then that a co-worker approached me with an interesting opportunity. A Hollywood publicist friend of his named Lisa was having a going away/birthday party to celebrate her departure to New York City and she wanted to have some porn stars there as eye candy. He mentioned that she ran with a pretty A-list crowd, so it might net some mainstream potential for the company if we played it right.

"I mean, Lisa is the kind of girl who winds up in the pages of *Star* by accident, and she knows everyone," he said. "Like, I remember one morning we went to brunch and midway through she slapped her forehead, saying, 'Oh shit! I'm supposed to be at the Kentucky Derby right now with Jerry Bruckheimer!' Know what I mean?"

I knew exactly what he meant and started thinking about the PR possibilities.

I met with the two of them later that week to discuss the logistics of it all. After a spirited story about how she woke up in Vegas after a night of drinking with a diamond engagement ring on her finger and no hint of a suitor, Lisa told me the details of her shindig. It was going to be poolside at the W in Westwood. She wanted at least one girl who was willing to work the crowd, so to speak, and one or two who were willing to be bathing beauties in the pool, kind of like mermaids. I did a mental rundown. Georgia was out of town, Angel was dancing (and would likely want to be paid), but Anais was around. She could do the crowd thing. And surely Mari and Flower would be into being bathing beauties? I made the suggestions.

"Great," she said. "I love it. And we're going to be doing gift bags too, so if there's anything you can think of that would be sexy to put in there..."

"Actually, one of the companies I work with can donate little pillow packs of lube called Moist."

"Perfect," she crowed. "The theme of the party is Wet Wednesday!"

"And another client I work with can donate some glow-in-the-dark vibrators," I added. "And, we can maybe give copies of the movie Anais was in that was featured in *Stuff* magazine?"

"That would be awesome! Thank you so much for this. Now, what can I do for you in return? Any way I can help?"

There was. I'd been trying for weeks to see if I could somehow get Anais going down the red carpet at the MTV Video Music Awards in Miami, just to say she was there for a PR stunt.

Unfortunately I was getting nowhere fast. All my contacts at MTV were failing me, and cold calling was just getting doors shut in my face. I asked her if there was anything she could do.

She thought for a moment, then, "Can you e-mail me her picture?"

I nodded. First thing the next morning I sent Lisa a handful of glamour shots. Two days later she e-mailed me back:

Your girl is in. The hook-up is at the Stuff Magazine party on Star Island, I'll get you all set up after we get my party out of the way.

Perfect. I bugged the Bosses for airfare and hotel, plus clothing expenses for Anais seeing as she'd have to have a smashing dress for the occasion. Meanwhile, I started prepping for the event at the W.

It went down on an uncharacteristically cold August evening. Anais was dressed in black pants and a purple satin top, her hair loose, her face nearly make-up free (despite my best efforts to encourage at least some eyeliner). Flower and Mari were all set to go, looking cute and beachy in their least rated bikinis. We all piled into our cars and caravanned to the W. Once we got there, Lisa jumped into action. She grabbed inner tubes and threw them into the pool, and after Mari and Flower stripped down in one of the cabanas, they hopped in the pool and started splashing around, sipping martinis the waiter brought them. Anais mingled with the crowd and charmed all the boys. Meanwhile, Lisa and I ran upstairs with some co-workers to finish stuffing the gift bags, of which one of two wire photographers took pictures.

Back downstairs it was mayhem. Mari and Flower were nowhere to be seen, and everyone was crowded into the far back corner of the pool area trying to stay warm near the heaters at the bar. Lisa asked me to get Mari and Flower back in the pool and attempted to pull the crowd to the other end of the pool, but to no avail. Lisa slipped her shoes off—I *knew* she was wearing Christian Louboutins!—and dunked her feet in the pool as one of the wire photographers joined us, taking shots of Lisa chatting with Mari and Flower floating around in their inner tubes.

"Can we take our tops off?" Mari called.

"Sure," Lisa told them. "Go ahead.

So they did. This got the attention of some of the party goers as a couple photographers took some shots of the topless, martini-drinking bathing beauties. I was starting to learn that Mari wasn't that shy after all. And at that point, the night was still young.

I was pulled this way and that, asked to meet this person, take care of Anais, get Mari and Flower back in the pool, entertain the talent manager who was hitting on Anais...everyone was pulling me this way and that. I was no longer a publicist, I was becoming a babysitter. My head was spinning and I needed a break. I went to The Backyard, the restaurant/bar that was adjacent to the pool, and sat next to Jamie Foxx, one of Lisa's invited guests. I was too exhausted to attempt to talk to him. I just needed a time-out.

As I made my way back up to poolside, my co-worker ran over to me and said, "You need to get Mari and Flower back into the pool. *Now.*"

"What's going on?" I asked, wondering how things could go horribly wrong in under fifteen minutes. He gestured to a cabana.

A cabana with the drapes closed.

A cabana packed with men, hooting and hollering, and flash-bulbs popping.

Oh fuck, I screamed inside my brain, positive that others heard me. This is why:

For most of us, we have a switch inside our brains that flips on and off from inappropriate to appropriate. We generally know when it should be flicked to appropriate—say, lowering your voice to say something dirty in a public place so only the intended recipient hears—and when it should be turned on inappropriate—like when you get too drunk in public and wind up in a heavy make-out session with your boyfriend in a club that makes most people uncomfortably whine that you should get a room, but really, big fucking deal. (Not that I know anything about that. But I digress.)

Porn girls do not have this switch. Rather, porn girls have a line. And what they do with it is jump in a Ferrari and burn rubber right over it as fast as they can—twice as fast if they've had a couple martinis.

For whatever reason—again, for some it's past abuse issues, for others it's not—most girls who become porn stars have been taught that the best way to get attention is by using sexual means. And to an extent most women learn this, except they don't take it to the extreme that adult industry workers do.

Where most women learn to use their feminine wiles by flirting and playing coy, maybe batting an eyelash and bending over while wearing something low cut, porn stars take it that extra 800 miles and go for the Full Monty with benefits. Near as I could tell, the girls got bored of not getting attention for being topless in the pool, so—not giving a moment's thought to where they were, who they were there with and what they were supposed to be doing—they decided to kick it up a notch.

I ran over to the cabana. As I tried to fight my way through the mass of dudes, two of them exited and high-fived each other, one telling the other that the girls were giving out free blow-jobs. I was told there were execs from NBC and Universal inside. Another guy exited the cabana and dared one of the guys waiting outside to smell his finger. Someone grabbed my arm and asked me to go check on Anais again. I was a fraction of a second away from screaming at them that clearly Anais wasn't the problem that needed tending to at that exact moment. I was beginning to lose my mind. I wanted a clone so I could be two places at once. As I debated what to do next (seeing as none of the guys were letting me break into their party), Lisa broke things up and I made my way inside.

"What's going on in here?" I asked.

Flower and Mari sat there, wrapped in towels, the picture of innocence. "Nothing," they chorused in unison.

"Bullshit. You're supposed to be outside in the pool."

"It's too cold," Mari whined.

"So put on some clothes and mingle," I hissed. "You're not here to give out free sex shows!"

"We weren't," Flower insisted. "Nothing was happening."

I was furious. There was no use in arguing with them because they weren't going to be honest with me about what was going on anyway. Lucky for them I was pulled away again, but demanded once more that they get out and mingle like they were supposed to. I spotted Lisa standing near the bar. The crowd had dissipated a fair amount, so I walked over to her to gauge how pissed she was.

"Lisa, listen," I started. "I'm sorry things got out of control—"

"I don't want to know what happened in there," she said, smiling tightly. "The less I know, the better."

Understood. I tracked down Anais, who was still being wooed by the talent manager, Garth. He asked if we'd be willing to go to dinner. I said maybe some other time. I was drained, and the thought that people I represented were ruining someone's party because they couldn't do the female equivalent of keeping it in their pants was making me ill.

Naturally, this was when I was told it was time to wrap it up. I looked toward their cabana. The curtains were closed again. I tore them open to find Flower, naked and crouching over top of a guy who worked at Paramount as his friend stood in the corner and watched next to Mari, who had her hand down the front of her swim trunks.

"Let's go. Right now," I said. They all looked at me like deer in headlights.

"*Now,*" I repeated angrily. I felt like their mom, which bothered the hell out of me considering they weren't that much younger than me.

The girls took their own sweet time putting their clothes back on and getting their shit together. The guys, despite my pleas, refused to leave, getting every bit of the free show they had hoped for. Finally I was free to leave. But I wasn't in any way, shape or form ready for the shitstorm that awaited me in the office the next morning.

One of the wire photographers had posted pictures of the girls' sexcapades on his website, which got picked up by Page Six who was threatening to run a newsbit on it. Lisa was melting down. And she let me know it loud and clear on the phone.

"I can't even believe this," she said, speaking so panicked that her words were running together. "I mean, what were you thinking!?"

I froze. "What was *I* thinking," I repeated.

"You let them swim in the pool topless!"

"No, they asked *you* and *you* said it was okay," I reminded her. I fully agreed their behavior was wrong, but there was no way in hell I was going to be blamed for it.

"I'm doomed," she moaned. "I've been kicked out of the W because they think I was trying to run some kind of brothel, and now I might as well not move back to New York. You don't know—I live a totally different life out there. I'm a socialite. I ice skate with Donald Trump, for chrissake!"

I was exasperated. On one hand, I could understand where Lisa was coming from. She called me asking to have porn stars play bathing beauties, not put on a live sex show in a poolside cabana. But on the other she'd encouraged them to go topless, and others encouraged them to push the envelope all the way to Timbuktu. And this was the problem with most people's approach to porn and the people who worked in it—they preferred to compartmentalize sexuality into little bite-sized pieces they could digest a little at a time while projecting their own hang-ups on others. The problem is, not everybody works that way—especially when they don't know what's going on in said person's head. So if those people in the industry didn't conform to those unspoken rules, they were looked down upon as lesser human beings. When I thought about it, in a way the girls were still private about their performance, hiding away behind the closed curtains of the cabana. At least they didn't take a raft into the middle of the pool and get it on in the great wide open.

I tried to calm her down to no avail. She wound up hanging up on me and spent the day instant messaging me about how her life was spiraling out of control because of *my* porn stars—as if I was some kind of crooked madam that had provided her with bunk entertainment and short-changed her on the finances. It was all fun and games until the porn stars started acting like porn stars.

Marlon Wayans

However, Lisa's wrath was nothing compared to that of Seymore Butts. On the way to work I'd called his assistant to relay the entire sordid tale of what I'd been through the night before as well as all that morning with Lisa, and she immediately called him to fill him in. Naively I believed that he would lay down the law, seeing as they were his contract girls. Oh, how wrong I was. When he called me to ask what was going on and I ran down my laundry list of complaints, he blamed me.

"Well where were you when this was going on?" he demanded.

"I was running around like a chicken with my head cut off," I shot back.

"On what—taking care of Anus?" (He liked to call Anais Anus. Actually, he liked to make up names for any clients I worked with that weren't either him or directly related to him.)

I ignored it. "Look, the point is they were told, explicitly, that they were there to swim in the pool... *not* that they were supposed to take over a cabana and put on a sex show for Hollywood bigwigs!"

"Do you know how much Mari had to drink that night?"

"No," I said. "I wasn't watching her every second of the night. I know I got her one at the beginning of the evening, and someone else got her another later on."

"She had at least four martinis that night," he said. "And Mari is a little girl!"

"She's also a fucking adult!" I spat. It infuriated me to no end that both he and Lisa were insisting that somehow I was to blame for their behavior, like I stopped using the remote control that made them behave and deliberately soaked it in the pool so it would malfunction and they'd start fucking each other with dildoes in plain view of a vacationing family looking out their third-floor window. I was a publicist, for fuck's sake. How did that make me responsible for people's personal malfunctions?

The answer was actually pretty simple in the end—there wasn't a lot of self-awareness in the porn industry, so it was much easier to blame people's shortcomings on others. To accept yourself and acknowledge your faults would mean looking further inward than most wanted to look, hence living in the fantasy world of the adult industry. But that was from the porn side of things. From the mainstream side, meaning Lisa, she just labored under the misapprehension that porn stars behaved like everyone else in social situations. I forgot to make it clear to her that most do, but some don't. I just didn't know at the time that I was representing some of the ones that don't.

Seymore wound up calming me down enough that he convinced me people talking about the party wasn't a bad thing that was probably spinnable, and talked me into giving Flower and Mari a second chance. Speaking of, they both started calling me repeatedly until Mari showed up unannounced at my office because I refused to answer the phone. We argued over their behavior, she demanded to call Lisa so she could explain what "really" went on, and I insisted she was the last person Lisa wanted to hear from. But Mari was upset. Mari wanted Lisa to know she wasn't a whore.

I appeased Mari for the moment and told her there was no use in dragging it out any longer. I advised her to let it go and told her I'd deal with it, which I did by writing a long letter to Lisa. I apologized on behalf of Flower and Mari for their behavior, but also pointed out that you couldn't have porn stars at a party and not expect them to act up. Of course, that didn't explain why Anais was so well-behaved, but that didn't matter. I wanted to make things better with Lisa. My co-worker told me she'd get over it and all would be well, but there was just one problem: she was my inroad to getting Anais on the VMA red carpet, and we'd already bought non-refundable plane tickets and paid for our hotel.

I made a snap decision. I'd already had us confirmed to attend some of the style villas and parties, which would be loaded with photographers and press. I decided we'd go anyway, armed with copies of her *Stuff*-reviewed DVDs, and somehow make it to the party on Star Island to get her on the red carpet. Add to that the fact that Garth had been e-mailing me to let me know he was going to be there too and he was willing to help. Though he had been e-mailing me strange missives asking questions about Chasey Lain's availability, I still took it as a good omen. When Lisa never e-mailed me back, my mind was made up. I called Anais and explained the situation: we were set for some high-profile parties that could get her coverage as well as a photo shoot with a wire service, but other than that, we'd have to rely on our own abilities to get her into the VMAs. Despite the appearance that her interest in the press game was waning, she assured me she was up for it.

In the meantime, Seymore subtly exacted his revenge on Mari. At the time that the pool party incident went down they were "on a break," but that didn't make Seymore any more comfortable with what did or didn't happen in that cabana. I got a heads up from his assistant that he was going to be calling me with some gossip, which he did. Apparently one night Mari went to a Hollywood club and hooked up, in the biblical sense, with one of the patrons there. Not that she took him home— no, she shagged him right there in the bathroom. Later that same night at the same club she met Marlon Wayans and went home with him to do the do. When all was said and done and Mari went home, Marlon apparently called a friend of his to brag about banging a porn star, which is when he discovered that said friend was the dude who banged her in the bathroom hours before.

"Are you saying you want me to run with this?" I asked.

"I'm saying I've given you the information," he said carefully, "and I'm saying you can do with it as you wish."

I knew what that meant. I called my contact at a highly-trafficked porn weblog to leak the information to them so it could be linked up and re-broadcast on Gawker Media's Fleshbot.com. They ran with it, more outlets picked it up, and someone mentioned to me that the *National Enquirer* even ran a blurb on it. I felt slimy about the whole thing, but what could I do? Seymore was one of my bosses, and his attitude was the more press the better, no matter what kind. What I did find interesting, though, is how Seymore had just given Mari a gift in the form of Julian, a big-dicked porn star she'd had a crush on for forever. Julian did her in the ass, Seymore taped it, and the whole episode was made into a scene for one of his movies. So it appeared to be okay for Mari to fuck other people in the relationship as long as Seymore approved. Of course, there were numerous unspoken rules in porn relationships that didn't translate to the real world. But that's another subject entirely.

The Music Industry Bigwig

There were other pressing issues at hand, though. I was starting to get a little worried about Anais' vetoing of media. Ever since she'd done the *VF*-esque photo shoot with a rich industry magnate, she'd been talking more and more about spending time with him, wanting to know about his past relationships, the girls he'd spent time with and the women he'd married. The more time she spent with him, the less she was interested in doing media-related things. I asked her point-blank if she wanted to slow down, but she said no, just that she wanted to be able to turn things down if she wanted. I took what she said at face value and continued full-steam ahead with plans for Miami and the VMAs.

But before we could go to Miami, we had to deal with the issue of her wardrobe. Ever the tomboy, Anais hated wearing anything other than shorts and tank tops from Hollister. I tried to explain to her that this wasn't a Hollister crowd—that she'd have to go a little more upscale if we were going to get her attention. Quickly she grew frustrated, yelling, "They should want to cover me because I'm a pretty girl. It doesn't matter what I wear!" So I stopped pushing. But then she started seeing my point when we sat down to discuss it and went through some of the magazines she wanted to be in someday. It helped when another industry publicist told her their girls had a clause in their contracts that stated they couldn't leave the house unless they looked like Britney Spears in case they were photographed. It was never my intent to force her into being something she wasn't, but unfortunately, it's all about image. And she had the image, she just had to refine it a little.

With that, we set out for Miami.

The night we left a fellow publicist friend offered to let me park my car at her place so she could drive us to the airport. As we waited to go, she grilled Anais on her hopes and dreams. Did she want to be a star?

"I don't know," she said noncommitally.

I pondered that, momentarily wondering why I was giving up four days of my life to go rub elbows with people who couldn't give a shit about who I was so that she could supposedly build a career, but it was too late. It was time to go.

Our hotel wasn't ready for us when we reached Miami, so we killed some time on the beach before checking in. A couple hours later we hopped in a cab heading to the Lowes suites, where we partook in freebies galore. Jelly shoes from Melissa. Hair clips and ceramic barrel round brushes from Helen of Troy, who tell us the Revlon iconic hair dryer is the best selling hair dryer on the market. T-shirts, tank tops and hats from New Era. Body art airbrushing kits that we wind up leaving at the airport days later because security wants us to dismember the impossible-to-open packaging to get the CO_2 cartridges out. The wire photographers take pictures of Anais with the merchandise. And nobody asked us who we were, nor did they seem to care. I felt slightly guilty, but at the same time I figured it would likely be the last shot I had at taking advantage of such an experience. So what the hell—we went for it.

While waiting for Anais to find the perfect-fitting pair of Buffalo jeans, Christina Milan walked out of the suite's bathroom wearing a different pair of Buffalos and a cute tank top. I told her I thought the jeans looked fabulous on her as she checked out the fit in the mirror. We engaged in conversation about the pain of finding jeans that fit well, have the right sized pockets, hug and flare in all the right places. I talked with Christina Milan not because she's famous and I dug her hit song at the time, I talked to Christina Milan because she was refreshingly personable. I could've cared less if she were a singer or a beggar. I couldn't say that was the same attitude everyone else in Miami had.

We headed back to the hotel with our bounty and made a quick change to attend Missy Elliot's Backyard BBQ at the Sagamore. We weren't on the list, but Garth—who called Anais when we were at the beach—offered to help out. I took a handful of Anais' DVDs plastered with stickers proudly proclaiming "As Seen In *Stuff* magazine October 2004!" as bribery just in case. They came in handy as we soon discovered Garth "forgot" to call us in and mysteriously stopped answering his cell phone for the rest of the weekend. Again, another not-uncommon occurrence. Hanging out with a porn star in L.A. with your buddy in a dark steak house was cool. Hanging out with her in front of A-listers in Miami? Potentially embarrassing. Best to avoid it. Funny how he e-mailed me nine months later wanting to know what was new, then suddenly disappeared when I made mention of his Miami dissing.

Anyway. Upon entrance I called some wire photographers I knew and warned them that we were there. They met us past the media wall at the stairwell. We hugged and kissed hello, but not in that fakey way that people do. They shot Anais in the stark white hallway leading out to the "back yard," which had a DJ spinning hip-hop and a buffet spread featuring hot dogs and hamburgers. They didn't care that Anais was a porn star. To them, she was a beautiful girl who modeled well and had star quality.

"Should we do some shots in front of the media wall?" I asked the photogs.

They smiled and nodded in agreement, leading Anais back down the hallway toward the wall advertising Missy's new clothing line and *Us* magazine. She walked in front of the wall and posed for them. A few other photographers followed suit as others watched, mouthing the words, "Who's that girl?" Behind me a cameraman said it out loud to the woman standing next to him.

"Nobody," she sneered. "It's a cute trick, though."

I debated not saying anything, but the devil on my shoulder made the smart-ass in me take over.

"Actually, I wouldn't say she's nobody just because you haven't heard of her," I said. I introduced myself as her publicist and ran down a list of accomplishments, including the magazines she was appearing in that fall. Admittedly, I glossed over the porn star information. I was certain it'd make her head implode.

"I didn't mean she's nobody as in nobody," the woman backpedaled. "I mean I hadn't heard of her."

"I know what you meant," I assured her. "Who do you work with?"

"I'd rather not say right now," she told me.

I wasn't surprised. I took a different line of questioning. "What kind of show?"

"Entertainment."

"Local?"

"No, national."

She wasn't in the mood to talk anymore. That was fine. I turned back to Anais who was walking back from the media wall and—having seen me chatting with the woman who worked for the national entertainment show with no name—held out her hand to the woman and introduced herself. The woman refused to shake it until she realized Anais wasn't going to retract her hand until pleasantries were exchanged. They shook and engaged in a little strained conversation. Anais sensed the resistance and turned to me. I was damn proud of her in that moment.

With that, we headed in for the BBQ. It was dead. Dead as a doornail dead. Pretty much nobody was there. Anais sniped about the absence of people, wondering aloud what kind of party I'd gotten her into. We hung out for a couple minutes, then decided that exhaustion had taken over and went back to the hotel where we had dinner, watched a little TV, then crashed out, skipping a Motorola party in favor of getting some rest.

The next morning we started out with a little breakfast and the beach before heading upstairs to change for our next party, a shindig put on by Lion's Gate at The Delano for the movie *The Cookout*. The whole thing was hosted by Queen Latifah. We were on the list for this one—that I knew for sure. It was confirmed long before we set foot on the plane to Miami. On our way there my photog friends called to warn us that they were running way behind—they wanted to shoot a series with Anais for the wire service they worked for—and advised us to cool our heels somewhere until they called us back. Anais started to complain, but I tuned her out and led her to Starbucks.

Too much caffeine later, we walked through The Delano to the back where the check-in tables were. I told them our names. They referred us to another table. I repeated the info. They referred us to yet another table. Lather, rinse, yadda yadda. Nope, we weren't listed there either. I tracked down the publicist for Lion's Gate and told him who added us and he confessed the entire party was a mess—even he didn't know who was on the list. Clusterfuck city. We opted not to expend precious energy trying other avenues and took a seat in the Blue Room, where we had salad and watched people arrive. Queen Latifah wore a smile that beamed from ear to ear. Farrah Fawcett looked frazzled and frail. The Wayans brothers wandered past. Word had it that earlier in the day, the party organizers were running so far behind that Diana Ross showed up on time for the shindig and was kept waiting for over an hour. She gave up and left before anything even began.

"You know," Anais said, mid-munch, "I love how you take me all the way out here and nothing is set up."

I froze. "Excuse me?"

"I mean…" she paused for a moment, back pedaling. "I thought we were on the list for this party?"

"We were," I said, shortly. "I had confirmation. I called the publicist, she said we were set, and now she's nowhere to be seen. Things like this happen, especially with events like the VMAs. Besides, we're just about to do a photo shoot with one of the wire services anyway."

She clammed up. Just then the photogs appeared, and we took a drive up the beach to a spot near their hotel. Anais stripped out of her jeans into a Roberto Cavalli bikini and started vamping as they snapped away. Comfortable being the center of attention again, she ate it up and gave them a stellar set. An hour and a half later they were finished and Anais was pleased with the results. I hugged them goodbye and we retired to the Style Villas at the Sagamore Hotel to hang out with a guy Anais met at Lisa's party. He was there with his company. He had money. Anais didn't leave his side for the rest of the afternoon until I practically had to tear her away from him to go back to the hotel to get ready for the evening. It was Saturday night, and it was time to execute our big plan: go to the *Blender* party, which we were confirmed for, to figure out how to sneak our way into the *Stuff* magazine Star Island party for Operation Red Carpet.

But first, she had to get dressed.

This was a two-hour ordeal.

Because I'd planned out my outfits before we left, getting ready was easy for me. Anais, on the other hand, was still wanting to wear tank tops and ratty jeans she had bought from Hollister.

I was exhausted from running around from place to place in the blazing hot sun, so I laid on the bed watching TV as she switched from tank top to tank top and vamped in the mirror.

After the umpteenth time, she asked me again: "What do you think?"

I sighed. "I don't care anymore," I said. And I meant it. She'd done nothing but complain with the exception of when we were hanging out with rich guys or when a camera was focused on her. At this point I just wanted whatever would make her happy so that I didn't have to hear it anymore.

"Oh, don't be like that."

"I'm not being like anything," I told her. "You already know what I think. I told you what I thought before we left home. Just wear what you want and let's go. I just want to get out of the hotel room now—I've been in here for too long."

She finally settled on a brown lace bustier and jeans, which looked great. We hopped in a cab and hit The Shore Club. Earlier in the day Anais had inadvertently picked up a bigwig modeling agency owner named Eddie who ran a company in Miami that represented girls like Gisele Bundchen. He took a major liking to her and we exchanged numbers so we could all hook up later. His friend, Buster, was standing outside of the *Blender* party when we got there, waiting to get in. When I finally tracked down the publicist because—once again—we weren't on the list (something Anais bitched at me about again), Buster attached himself to us as our third. He thanked us for letting him tag along and mentioned he was going to meet a friend of his, Breakfast, to get to the *Stuff* party on Star Island.

I asked him if he could help us get into it. He told us it'd be no problem. Anais smiled at me and we high-fived. Mission accomplished.

Or so I thought.

The first people we meet are Girls Gone Wild proprietor Joe Francis and his bodyguard. I spent time chit-chatting with the bodyguard, who told me how he became a part of the company and how he lived in Japan for a while. He pointed out this producer and that actor and made introductions. We all had fun talking about porn. I had some much-needed laughter. In the corner sat Jessica Simpson and Nick Lachey with their posse eating sushi. The bodyguard and I paused conversation to watch the Olsen twins walk in. They were even tinier in stature than they seem in magazines—three apples high would be pushing it—and they looked like frightened little birds. I almost felt sorry for them and their kazillions. I grabbed some wire photographers and get them to take shots of Anais, which they did, much to her chagrin. They asked what she did. She cut me off and told them she was a model before I could get the "p" word out of my mouth. People asked for product. I handed them cards. As Anais disappeared to the rest room, guys swarmed me with a flurry of chatter.

"Is Anais single?"

"Tell Anais I think she's hot."

"I had a lovely time talking to her, is she free tomorrow?"

Despite me telling them that Anais could certainly speak for herself, could handle compliments and makes her own schedule, they continued to bombard me with queries and heartfelt desires as if I owned the key to the lock on her low-slung jeans. I was no longer a publicist. I was a pimp. I discovered it was a role I wasn't comfortable with.

Speaking of pimp, right around that time Anais' eyes bulged out of her head as a guy walked past. She tugged my arm. "Do you know who that is?" she asked.

I shook my head.

"That's Jordan Schur."

I shrugged.

"He, like, owns Universal or Geffen records or something," she said, eyes gleaming.

"Oh." I was unimpressed.

"I know him."

"How?" I asked.

"Well, my cousin took me to the Playboy mansion when I was 17, and I met him there," she said. "So for a while I was kind of living with him and he was paying me, like, a thousand a week not to do porn."

"He was paying you *not* to do porn?" I repeated.

She nodded.

I wasn't stupid—I knew what that meant. The retired starlet's words rang in my ears, and it all started to make sense: the constant interest in rich guys, the waning interest in promotion opportunities, and how her good time in Miami hinged on whether or not she was spending it with a dude who was loaded. So I wasn't the least bit surprised when she pulled Jordan aside and, after a few minutes of chatting, told me she was going to go talk to him in private for a little while. That's when Buster and Breakfast came up and warned me that the limo for Star Island was leaving in 20 minutes, so if Anais and I were going we'd have to be out front on time or else it was leaving without us. I watched the time tick down on my cell-phone clock as skinny, coked-out starlet after beefy, self-absorbed wanna-be wandered past. I peeked outside to see Jordan and Anais still talking animatedly by the media wall as if they were having an argument, until the cameras started snapping and filming them. Luckily the limo was running late—Buster stopped by to warn me, and I could still see a flash of Breakfast's platinum-blond hair moving through the crowd. After an hour Anais finally returned.

"I'm leaving with Jordan," she told me.

"What? Why?" I asked even though I knew the answer.

"Because we're going to talk things over. We have some stuff to discuss."

"But we have the party on Star Island! This is the whole reason why we're here!" Even I knew it was a lame attempt at that point, but I had to try.

Jordan interjected, pulling out a mitful of wristbands from his pocket. "Is it one of these? I've got one for every party in Miami this weekend. Seriously." He disappeared.

Anais gave me a look that said there was no way in hell she was going to Star Island with me.

"We're trying to get you to go to the awards," I said.

"If it weren't for Jordan there wouldn't be any awards!" she cried.

"Is Jordan going to take you to the awards tomorrow?" I asked.

"Probably." Jordan reappeared again and told Anais the limo was ready. She waved to me.

"Be safe," I told her, then went to look for Buster. He was gone.

On the way home I got a call from Eddie asking where Anais was. When we'd met him earlier in the day Anais had been cagey with him about her profession, deciding against telling him she was a porn star because he was fawning over her so much and wanting to set up a meeting with her Monday morning to potentially rep her. At the time I'd thought I'd keep the porn under wraps so it wouldn't spook him. But at that point, I didn't care. I was likely going to be fired when I got home for not getting Anais on the red carpet like I'd promised, so I had nothing to lose.

"She's gone," I told him.

"Where?"

"She took off with Jordan Schur and left me here."

"That's not nice to do to a friend," he said.

"She's not a friend, she's a client," I corrected him. "And I'm a big girl. I can fend for myself."

"I can't say that I'm interested in signing her if this is how professional she is with her publicist," he said. "What is it she does again? Modeling?"

"She's a porn star, Eddie."

"A *porn star*? Unbelievable. She's trashy. What a horrible career choice."

I found it interesting that Anais was gorgeous and had a huge future ahead of her until Eddie found out she was in porn.

"What are you doing now?" he asked.

"I don't know. I was trying to get to Star Island, but that ship has sailed without me."

"It sucks anyway. Come meet me at Rokbar."

"Let me see how I feel—I'm kinda tired," I said.

"Just come. It'll be fun."

"I tell you what—if I'm coming I'll call you within an hour and let you know, okay?"

That was okay with Eddie. He gave me the name of the bouncer and hung up. I contemplated my options and decided bed was the best one. Eddie called me again at 4am to see where I was, but I didn't answer. When I looked next to me in bed I realized I was alone.

Around 6am Anais walked in the door. I opened one eye.

"Sorry, I didn't want to wake you," she whispered.

"Are you okay?"

"Yeah. Jordan and I just talked all night. But check this out—he gave me money for a cab home. I didn't know how much it was, he just slipped it into the back pocket of my jeans. So I go to pay the driver and look what I pull out!" She shows me a huge wad of hundreds. "There's over two thousand dollars here!"

Talked all night, I thought. If I'd had the energy I would've rolled my eyes. I turned over and went back to sleep.

I got up a couple hours later and went for breakfast alone, leaving Anais in bed to recuperate. I start thinking about how I'd failed my bosses and how I wished Anais would've just told me she wasn't interested in doing any of this rather than going along with everything so I could waste my weekend. I ignored it all because nothing mattered when I decided to shut my brain off and go shopping for things I most certainly didn't need but was sure that I wanted, despite the fact that my suitcase was already overflowing and I refused to check my luggage at all costs. I tried on shoes. That was my zen moment after a weekend of insanity. Anais called me to tell me she was at the beach. I met her after I was done racking up my credit cards.

Although I didn't want to push her, part of me wanted to know if she was going to admit to me that she didn't want anything to do with the whole VMA plan. So I asked her if she was going to go to the show with Jordan. She was non-committal, then made plans with the rich dude from the Sagamore Style Villas. They were going to do dinner at The Shore Club before hitting Usher and Diddy's after parties. I opted to do dinner with media friends and told her I'd meet up with her later, but in the meantime, "throw yourself in front of the path of every camera you can."

She laughed. I knew she wasn't going to do it. And I wasn't surprised when she didn't pick up her phone when I called her after dinner so I could join the after-parties. Fine by me, I needed the sleep anyway. The next morning I started packing and organizing the hotel room. Our plane left at 4pm, and by noon she still wasn't at the hotel. I called her cell and left a message: "I'm not mad, I'm not going to chew you out. Just call me and let me know you're okay and when you're coming home to pack." I hung up. She called me two seconds later and told me she would be home in an hour. We caught our flight on time. When my friend picked us up from the airport I burst into tears. I was so worn out. I drove like Andretti all the way down the 405 and 101 back to my place so Anais could pick up the rest of her stuff, then motored her over to her cousin's place. She didn't want to be promoted. I'd wasted my time. That was fine, though—I understood that people changed their minds. I would just give her space so that she didn't feel pressured by me anymore.

by Olivia, Carly, Amanda, and Jennifer

David Bowie, Prince and John Tesh

Once I got home, I called the retired star who had told me about Anais' escorting excursion.

"You were right," I told her. "She hooks."

"Told you so," she said. "Anyone famous?"

I relayed the tale of how she and Jordan hooked up at the *Blender* party. She laughed.

"Typical Jordan," she said.

"He's done this before?"

"Oh, all the time. He loves keeping porn stars as pets. In fact, he once offered to do the same for me, and I passed. I just wasn't interested. But yeah, he's always up for that kind of stuff. And usually the younger, the better."

I asked her if she'd ever been with anyone famous. She told me about the time she spent a week with David Bowie in Vancouver in the early 80s ("I think it was during his China Girl phase...he was great.") and the time she had the opportunity to hook up with Prince ("I was at a bar and he sent his people over to come get me and deliver me to him, but I told them if he wanted to talk to me he could come on over...when his people told him what I said, he shook his head sadly and left. I've kicked myself ever since!"), but the most surprising celebrity encounter had no sex whatsoever and happened at a movie theatre.

"I was standing in line to pay for my ticket or get popcorn or something, and I looked over to see John Tesh and Connie Sellecca," she told me. "He approached me and said, 'Are you...' and I told him yes, I was, and very excitedly told me, 'I love your movies—I'm a really big fan!' Who would've thought! John Tesh!"

I laughed. I thanked her for chatting with me, but it was time for me to get off the phone. I had to try and get some sleep.

The next day at work I gave the bosses the rundown of the whole Miami ordeal. They were pissed. Of course, when they met with Anais she told them a completely different story that finished with her teary desire to quit the industry—she was concerned about what her daughter would think of her—coupled with tales of how I was a horrible taskmaster who wanted to sleep with her. When I was accused of this, all I could do was laugh.

In retrospect it made sense that Anais was telling people that I'd made a play for her action. The entire time I'd been working with her she'd constantly told me about this guy and that guy who was hot for her. She'd told me an incredibly long and involved story about the production manager that painted him out to be a desperate pursuer, when in actuality it was the other way around. Hal Sparks asking her for her phone number? Never happened. In reality, Anais—beautiful as she was—was wholly insecure and needed the constant attention, both male and female, to feel worth. It was the accusation about me that made me realize it, prompting me to ask around the office to all the people she claimed hit on her to get their real stories. Suddenly her entrance to the world of porn made sense. What better way to feel wanted and needed in short order than by becoming a sex symbol the easy way? At that point I no longer felt exasperated over the whole work situation with her—I just felt sad that she couldn't find something within herself to make her feel worthy. And I was happy that she'd recognized it, likely inadvertently, and gotten out of the industry as a result.

Most girls only last in the industry a couple of years, then disappear to do something else with their lives. It's tougher on girls in porn than it is for escorts or even mainstream actresses in terms of their supposed market value. Putting your body through so much sex can be taxing and aging, and there's no hiding it on videotape. Porn stars who want to sustain a career have to straddle the line between over-exposure and having a healthy body of work all the time...but the number of women who become a household name is small. Although their time in the industry is immortalized on video and it's likely people will find out what they did, most figure out ways to move on from their on-camera career in one way or another. Some work behind the scenes in the industry, either on-set on in an office. Others make a complete career change. I knew of one former stud who was working on getting his Real Estate license, while a former contract star was set on her dreams of being a veterinarian, and another was content working as a waitress in a bar far, far away from Los Angeles. And then there's always the option of marrying rich, where the girls find a sugar daddy, have kids, and become a housewife for the rest of their lives. Anais reportedly had bigger plans. She stopped by the office to get copies of her favorite stills from photo shoots she'd done. She was planning on becoming a model.

A couple weeks later, my friend Cly Maxwell alerted me to her listing on one of the top escorting sites—one where patrons had to prove they made a minimum of six figures in order to be a member. Though many of the girls who escorted preferred to work alone, others flocked to this site to not have to worry about anything but showing up somewhere on time to have sex for money. Tons of name girls from the industry worked with this site, which took a percentage of their earnings for hooking them up on "dates" with everyone from successful businessmen to members of the FBI. The pictures Anais had gotten from the office were the same ones that ran along with her listing. So much for that mainstream modeling career. Idly, I wondered what her daughter would think of that.

Gene Simmons and Scott Baio

The Hollywood bleed-over was proven to me once again when I threw a party in Las Vegas during the 2005 Adult Entertainment Expo. The Adult Entertainment Expo showcases adult companies and their stars for five days every January at the Sands Hotel. Fans come from all over the country to see their favorite porn girl in person, and the whole event is capped by the AVN Awards, porn's version of the Oscars.

This year had all the usuals in attendance (Lemmy from Motorhead; Steven Tyler, who supposedly left a Consumer Electronics Show party for Playstation to attend mine; Mike Tyson, a staple at events like this) and some interesting but bizarre additions (Huey Lewis, and club management told me Jeffrey Katzenberg had requested a table.) Seeing celebrities at the Adult Entertainment Expo was nothing new—year before last, Vin Diesel was reportedly seen wandering the aisles incognito with his handlers (though many insist it was to combat the rampant gay rumors at the time), and David Spade once made a memorable appearance wherein he dropped his pants in front of a company's booth, giving him a one-way ticket off the show floor.

So it was nothing new to see a throng of people, photographers, camera crews and security making their way down the aisle, except this time they were headed directly for my company's booth. As the crowd parted to allow the person through to the private conference room, I saw who it was: Gene Simmons, the demon himself from KISS.

He walked toward the booth entrance. I stood aside to let him through. He fixed me with a steely gaze as he came to a dead stop in front of me. He didn't move. He just kept staring.

Not knowing what to do, I stuck out my hand and said, "Hi, Mr. Simmons. My name is Carly and I'm the publicist for this company."

He gripped my hand with his and pulled me into him as he put his arm around my shoulders and led me into the conference area. "Carly," he said, his nose nuzzling my ear. "Do you know that you're the hottest girl here?"

I smiled. "That may be, Mr. Simmons, but I'm also the most taken girl here."

Instantly his arm was removed from my shoulders as he announced, "Then I have no interest in you." And he sat on the couch in the conference area as porn girl after porn girl entered and crawled all over him.

I laughed. It was vintage Gene from what I could tell. A porn director friend had once told me a great story about the time he met Gene at a show his wife's band was doing at the House of Blues. He'd shown up with his favorite Kiss album readied for an autograph and started reciting a speech about what an honor it was to meet him when Gene cut him off to tell him how hot his wife was and how much he'd like a piece of her. A week later Gene called the director's wife at work, and she called him to report the conversation.

"Gene Simmons just called me to ask me if I could spend a night with him," she said.

"You tell Gene Simmons he can spend a night with you if I can spend a night with Shannon Tweed," he shot back.

Dutifully, she called Gene to tell him this. And then she called her husband back.

"So what did he say?"

"He said absolutely not, and hung up."

The director friend always had great stories to tell about his time in the industry, but one of my favorite stories of his had to be the time Scott Baio was on one of his sets. He'd shown up to work late and hung over, certain he was hallucinating Scott Baio on his set. But after he'd gotten used to it, as they shot their movie throughout the day he and Scott got into a discussion about whether or not you could really write a script about anything and make a porno out of it in 24 hours. The director insisted it could be done. Scott wasn't so sure.

"It can," the director said defiantly. "In fact, I can go home tonight and write a porn script about leprosy and shoot it tomorrow if I want to."

"No way," Scott scoffed.

"I'll bet you ten dollars."

They shook on it. And true to his word, the director wrote his leprosy script and shot it the next day. When the movie came out, he sent it to Scott.

"Did you ever get your ten bucks?" I asked.

"No," he grumbled. "Scott Baio is a deadbeat in my books."

Anyway. Not long after the 2005 Expo I wound up leaving the industry behind. Some people I kept in touch with, others I didn't. But the one person I did hear from, much to my shock, was Lisa. Exactly a year after the W debacle and five months after I'd left the industry, she text messaged me:

Hi Carly it's Lisa! It's my birthday again and I'm throwing another party, this time in The Hamptons. Do you have any girls that need some exposure?

I laughed until my insides were sore. Clearly her life wasn't as ruined as she'd made it out to be... at least, not so much that she wasn't willing to have porn stars attend her birthday again. Funny how that happens. I texted back:

Sorry, I'm outta the game. Have a good birthday.

I never heard from her again.

Amanda

A Day in the Life

I saw a regular client this morning at 6:30. He's mega-rich, sixty-something, involved in the film business in some way—an agent or producer or something. Married of course. I see John every other week at his "office," which is really a luxury condominium in Beverly Hills, several miles away from his mansion on Sunset Boulevard. A true type-A personality, John always books me for 6:30am. That's the best time to squeeze me in— he tells his wife he's going off to early-morning yoga.

As soon as I walked through the door of his condo I could tell he was in a very bad mood. John was sitting at his desk with all the lights on the phone flashing, screaming at the top of his lungs about a big deal that had gone wrong and somebody who had screwed him over. He was heart-attack furious. When he hung up I told him I could see the morning wasn't going smoothly for him and offered to come back at a better time. He calmed down, slightly, saying "No, no, this has nothing to do with you...I'll be with you in a minute...just let me make one more call."

He then proceeded to call some poor person who worked for him and just berate the guy. Bellowing horrible accusations at some poor man on the other end, who sat and took it. When he tried to defend himself my client just screamed louder. "You're have shit for brains! Everything you do is wrong! I'm the only person who ever thinks—I have to do everything! Why should I have to pay some idiot asshole to fuck everything up!" On and on. I could hear the poor guy on speakerphone; he was quickly reduced to just saying, "I'm sorry, I'm sorry."

When he finally slammed down the phone again I said, very politely, "You really should be on Prozac or Xanax or some sort of mood stabilizer. I think it would help you."

John took great offense at my well-intentioned remark. "Who the fuck are you to say something like that to me?"

"Honey, I'm just concerned. Every time I see you you're screaming at someone. You can't talk to people that way."

"Fuck *you*!" he screamed.

I grabbed my Louis Vuitton carry-all with the tools of my trade (condoms, Rigaud candles, massage oil, scented sanitary wipes, lubricant) stood up and started walking. "John, I can't imagine why you think you can talk to *me* that way. Maybe others will put up with it, but I certainly don't have to. Good-bye." I wasn't kidding. I may be a call girl, but I don't have to put up with this kind of disrespect. I don't care how many billions he has or how powerful he is at some studio.

John came up behind me and grabbed my hand. "I'm sorry honey, you just can't imagine the kind of morning I'm having… those fucking idiots on the set…." On and on he went.

"Again, John, I will be happy to come back at a better time."

"No, baby, please stay...." He pulled me toward the bedroom. "I'm sorry, honey, I'm just so tense..."

I put a little pout on my face and started speaking in semi-baby-talk. "John, look, I got all pretty for you this morning, now can't we just forget about business for an hour? Stop thinking about work, I'm here to have a good time with you now." I led him into the bedroom and started massaging his back. Eventually I managed to calm him down completely. I gave him a great rub-down, sucked his dick for awhile and eventually we had basic, boring sex—which is to say it all turned out fine. I got my usual $500 cash and was in and out the door in less than an hour. But as I drove away my head was pounding. I realized just how tired of this kind of shit I really am. Tired of men like these, where the whole world has to revolve around them. They can't imagine a life where everything isn't all about them. They're ass-holes, pretty much.

And deep down they're all the same. All these Fortune 500 jerks. *What*, I want to ask them, *is so special and important about your life?* When their dry-cleaning isn't ready at 8am their whole day is ruined. If they can't take off in their private plane the second they want to it's an earth-shaking catastrophe. That never-ending finger-snapping and barking and thinking that everyone on earth is here to do their bidding. My God, the constant babying and reassuring and coddling you have to do for some of these men. Actual sex is the least demanding part of my job—all this other crap is what gets so draining and makes me realize for the hundredth time that I have to get out of this business.

But I've been doing it for almost twenty years now. When I really stop to think about that fact—*I'm forty, and I've been doing this for half my life*…I can't believe it. Like every other girl I've ever known in this game, I always say, "I'm getting out. Next year, for sure." But the reality is that I've been saying that for fifteen years. The reality is that sex for money is the business I've chosen. It's what I do. The difference between me and the majority of the many other call girls I've known is that I've been smart about it. I haven't pissed away all my money on drugs and clothes and trips and cars. I am a true businesswoman and run my own small business like a professional. And that's why I've lasted this long.

Rule #1 in any business is to not let people walk all over you. Once you let a man treat you like dirt, they will push it as far as they can. Certain men will demean you to the point where you start to think of yourself like they do—just a hooker. And that's a place I will not go. I've been in this game a long time and I've known hundreds of crazy men. But the bottom line is that every client must treat me with a certain level of respect, as one professional to another.

Here's an interesting fact I would never have believed when I was 25: At age 40, I'm busier now than I've ever been. I am here to tell you that men—and I mean rich, powerful, attractive men—don't necessarily want to have sex with the youngest, hottest girl there is. I make an excellent living with regular clients—many of them I've had for ten years. I don't do anal sex. I don't do drugs. I've never had plastic surgery, and I don't pretend to be some wild kinky partier. Yes, I stay in shape and take good care of myself, and I was certainly blessed with good looks to start…but the long and the short of it is that I am a good businesswoman. I provide what men want—and that's a lot more than looks.

The Game

I grew up in the small California beach town of Dana Point, close enough to Hollywood to get bitten by the acting bug. I had classic California-beach-girl looks and plenty of attention from men from an early age. I came from a prominent, loving family—my father is a respected cancer researcher; my mother raised the kids and did charity work. As a young girl I would never have dreamed that "call girl" would be my chosen profession.

I had fantasies of being in the movies for awhile, so that's why I moved to L.A as soon as I got out of college. I took acting classes and dabbled with going on auditions and casting calls. I soon encountered a number of powerful men in the business via the casting couch. I heard plenty of promises about how I could be the next big thing. That I could get this or that part provided I was "easy to work with." I understood what that meant. I hated it. I wasn't going to have sex with somebody to catch a break. After seeing how the movie business really worked—at least the casting sessions I saw—I lost interest in acting as a profession. Sex for money I could understand—that seemed like a much more honest business transaction to me. But to sleep for free with gross middle-aged men for the chance of—maybe—one line on a stupid sitcom? No way.

I didn't have to be talked into anything when a girlfriend introduced me to Madam Alex, who was at that time at the height of her power and influence. This was back in the day when the whole high-class call girl business was in full swing. I was young, I was adventurous, I never wanted to be or do anything average. I was never looking to marry the nice guy next door. I liked older men...still do.

Madam Alex was a very strange woman—quite intimidating to a young girl. My girlfriends and I used to call her the spider; she used to live in her bed with the phone to her ear spinning her webs all over town. She was a straight-up hard cold business-woman. And she was picky about who worked for her. She wanted her girls to all conform to a certain standard. They had to be young and fresh-looking—not hard. Very little makeup, modest clothes…she had very specific standards for any girl who wanted to go on a job for her.

I was so young the first time I met Madam Alex that I didn't even understand any of the business part of all this. I was in an earthy stage; I never cared what my hair looked like; I used to wear peasant skirts and tank tops and sandals everywhere; no makeup, inexpensive turquoise and silver jewelry. I favored the hippie look, but I was so young that it didn't matter. I was pretty and soft-spoken, the furthest thing from a hard-bitten call girl imaginable. I was exactly what Madam Alex was looking for. Young, innocent, a certain lack of sophistication. The last girl you would ever imagine had sex for money.

My first job seemed like fun. I was booked with three other girls—one was the friend who had taken me over to Madam Alex's house to introduce me. We got sent as a group to Adnan Khashoggi's mansion in Santa Barbara, where he was throwing a party. His gated estate was right next to Nixon's, and it was fabulous. One of the princes there took an immediate liking to me, because I didn't do drugs. I wasn't much of a drinker, and I didn't even smoke cigarettes! It was a very decadent scene—major hard partying going on all over this estate, so I immediately stood out. This particular Arab prince appreciated a girl who wasn't stoned out of her mind.

I was a guest at that party for less than three hours. I had sex with the prince, one of Khashoggi's guests, in a luxurious guestroom. It was easy; it was more or less the kind of sex I would have had on a date. The Prince was adoring and kind and certainly didn't want anything kinky. And I walked out that door with an obscene amount of money— $2500 cash.

My three girlfriends and I drove back to L.A. together that night, laughing and giggling and drinking from a bottle of Dom Perignon we had taken home with us. Combined, we had $10,000 cash in our hands! I had never imagined seeing that much money in my life. I told my girlfriend, "I can't believe how easy that was!" "What did I tell you?" she said. "It's fun!"

The way it worked was that the client—Khashoggi in this case—paid the girls, who gave Alex their cut after the job. Alex took a 40% commission, and she was a very paranoid woman. At times she believed her house was being watched, so there was always a prearranged time the girls could stop by to drop off the cash. Alex was always talking on the phone when I went in to hand over the money. She would keep talking as she counted it and then wave me away, dismissing me until the next time she called.

I was so naïve that it never even entered my mind to try and cheat her, though over the years I'm sure some girls tried. I could tell right away she was nobody to fool with. I had no doubt she would have immediately tracked down any girl who tried to keep her money and have her killed. I had no desire to cheat her anyway—I was making plenty of money! I didn't begrudge Alex her 40%. She, of course, was just raking in the cash; there were stacks and stacks of hundreds hidden all over her place.

I remember sitting on my bed alone at home in my little apartment in West L.A. that night, just staring at the fifteen $100 bills in my hand. That kind of experience will ruin you for life if you let it. The easy money was just too easy. Prostitution is an addiction like any other, and every other woman I know in this business will say the same thing. It's always so easy and harmless the first time. And the thrill of that cash is impossible to resist. I am an addict, like many call girls I know, in thrall to the business. I talk about quitting all the time. I say I can stop anytime I want but never do. Just like an addict.

Madam Alex's Girl

This profession can really fuck a girl up. And looking back, I admit it's fucked me up residually, for sure. I could never, ever trust any man. 99.9 percent of the men I've been with were cheating on their wives. And if the man has money—sorry, make that 100%. I hate to sound so jaded, but I think I'm just realistic. If you take someone rich or famous, there's no way they're faithful. Men cheat, I know this, believe me. We are talking established, good-looking men with beautiful, intelligent wives. Maybe it's a bit of that whole virgin/whore complex—they want a gorgeous wife to stay home, raise nice children, give great dinner parties and entertain important guests, but they also want to fuck a bad girl. They don't want to *marry* a bad girl, but they sure like having sex with one. So— they find a call girl. Most of my clients are quite happily married! They say so, and I believe them. My average client is in a solid, long-term marriage to a lovely wife, with a couple of kids.

I'm certainly not saying the call girl life is for everyone; I understand girls who become alcoholics and drug addicts because of the lifestyle. The nineties in L.A. were wild...and there were many casualties. I was young and sweet, but I had a certain street-smarts about me all along. I was determined not to be one of them.

Madam Alex and I got along very well, and I never went looking for business anywhere else. I started seeing all of her regular clients, which, in the nineties, meant a lot of famous people. I did meet Heidi Fleiss on several occasions, with whom Madam Alex had a love/hate relationship, but I never worked for her. The first time I was introduced she was in a bar surrounded by a few of her girls; she asked me if I wanted to go on a quick job for some writer guy named Roger Friedman. The girls were laughing and saying they didn't want to go; he was rumored to be a lousy lay and cheap besides. It didn't sound like my kind of thing; I politely turned her down. I just wasn't her type of girl; I was too soft, not aggressive enough. She never asked me to work for her again, but I didn't care; I knew plenty of Heidi's girls and wasn't that impressed. Lots of drugs and drama. I had all the business I could handle from Madam Alex alone.

Charlie Sheen

I had a professional relationship with Charlie Sheen before he married Denise Richards. (Many girls did!) I saw him all the time, he was one of my regulars. Me and three or four other girls—he used to call us all the time. And this is what I have to say: Charlie Sheen was a lot of fun. He was very boyish, out to have a good time. He was never degrading or abusive to us. He was a good kisser, a good lover, an all-around good time.

He had a naughty little-boy side. He was so fun, just a great client. People say he's a sex addict or maniac or whatever... but I never thought so. He just loves women. He likes everything about them. He has a lot of variety in his character, and he likes a lot of variety, sexually. Sometimes I'd dress up in a skimpy cheerleader outfit for him; he enjoyed fantasies. He liked two girls together, three girls together...you name it, he liked it. But through it all he had a sensual quality that was very appealing...he wasn't just a rabbit fucking you. He used to actually talk to me and we would have intelligent conversations about all kinds of things. He liked younger girls too, eighteen or nineteen, and he loved to get down on their level and play. But he never talked down to anyone. Ever.

Of course back in those days he was deeply into cocaine and alcohol, and he has since cleaned up his act. I'm sure sobriety really did clear his head, and I'm equally sure he fell madly in love with Denise and got married. She's a beautiful woman, I'm sure he was anxious to grow up a bit, settle down, raise a family, not act like a perpetual adolescent. Now, I certainly wouldn't presume to know anything about the reasons for their nasty split, but it was said that gambling was involved. Though I'm not sure you leave your husband when you're pregnant over *gambling*. I imagine it was another woman in some way. And I feel bad about all the beating he's taking in the press about his ugly divorce, because he was always such a good guy that I truly wish him the best and hope he is happy. He was an absolute sweetheart, and it would be very sad if he were to fall back into the whole scene again. But an addict is an addict, and all the vices are interrelated: sex, gambling, smoking, alcohol, drugs... it's a slippery slope.

The Freak

Not all clients were as easy as that. Take the head of a huge advertising agency with a flagship building on the Sunset Strip in Hollywood. How I'd love to use his real name so everyone would know what a *freak* he is, but honestly, it doesn't matter. To the general public, he's a nobody—that is, not an actor or famous—but he was very, very important in his own mind. He set all his appointments at his office; it was part of his control thing. He was waaaaay into S&M, domination and control, and I was the one being dominated. He used to sneak me in through a back door and hide me in a closet, handcuffed. He loved the anticipation of a helpless girl cowering in the closet while he was barking orders at his secretary on the other side of the wall. It wasn't such a bad closet, actually, it was quite nice, as closets go. More of a little room, I would say.

He would leave me locked in the closet for a long time, while he finished dictating letters and making calls. I was supposed to be scared, of course, so I pretended to be terrified, though I really wasn't. He really got off on the image of the pretty, petrified girl helpless in his closet and enjoyed letting the anticipation build. Finally, after his secretary and all the other office staff left, he would come and release me from the closet. He'd tell me he'd found some black hookers downtown that he was bringing over to fuck me, the most vile women he could find. I would remain blindfolded while he related all these elaborate fantasies about gross diseased whores—"She going to have to do whatever I say! Or whatever you tell her to do!" The language would get really vile, and I would just sort of go along with it. "Ummmm...OK...whatever you say." No other woman was ever really there. It was his sick fantasy, and he never tired of it.

Then he'd pull my hair, smack me around a little, get a bit rough. There was a special code word I could use if things got too out of control, and he would stop, but I never had to use it. I was never that afraid, though I pretended to be. I usually just endured these sessions.

One day he told me that he had a special surprise for me. He brought me into his office as usual, blindfolded and handcuffed. When he removed my blindfold I saw a skinny, shivering crack addict there in front of me. She was a young black girl named Letice; she was right off the corner of Alvarado. I realized for sure that this man had crossed the line; he was completely whacked out to take his fantasies this far. I was not anxious to touch her, or let her touch me, for that matter.

He kind of pushed her around, called her a piece of shit, a low-rent crack whore, that kind of stuff. He put the blindfold on her and told me, "She's our toy tonight...we can beat the shit out of her if we want to!" He was very excited. "You're going to fuck this black whore now!" he told me after he got good and worked up. This was one time I really *was* a little afraid of him. I said, "Sure, sure," and went over to the girl. I whispered in her ear, "Just go along with whatever I say and do...I'm not going to hurt you." I played along as much as I could, pretend-slapped her face a few times, called her a few names, and basically talked dirty. Then Letice gave him a blow-job and he came all over her face.

Once he had his orgasm, he was Mr. Straight Normal guy again. But after that night, I swore to myself, "Never again." He was just a freak; he used to talk about fucking little twelve-year-old girls and making them his slaves.... Now, fantasies are fantasies, and many people have them but would never act on them. I really had the feeling with this guy that if he got the chance, he would enslave a thirteen-year-old girl and beat her, fuck her, and abuse the hell out of her. This man had no heart. I never saw him again.

Candy Spelling

Frankly, and I can only give my own personal opinion, I think Aaron Spelling was gay. All those lawsuits against him for sexual harassment were just crap, because I don't think the man really swung that way. His wife, too, is certainly not altogether straight. That I do know for a fact.

Aaron knew a girl in the business and that's where I came in… he was looking to do something nice for his wife. He really, truly loved her. Back in the nineties I saw Candy Spelling nine or ten times over a year or so. And it was great. Every time I went to their huge Bel-Air mansion there would be champagne waiting for me on a silver tray. Caviar, servants. Music. What Aaron Spelling wanted was for his wife to have a good time, but he certainly enjoyed watching his wife with another woman.

Candy Spelling was the nicest, kindest woman imaginable. Both of them were very generous to me. Candy was in her fifties at the time, still beautiful, and clearly no novice. Not that I think she was with other women all the time, but she had been down this road before and clearly liked it.

The setting, of course, was incredible. I only went to one wing of the estate, but everything I could see was gorgeously decorated. Flowers, beautiful linens, Jacuzzi baths and heated towels, candles…. It wasn't cheap and nasty and gross…not dildoes and dirty talk and crotchless underwear. Actually, it was a very elegant affair. Kissing, massaging, culminating in me going down on her while her husband watched. As the finale they would make love while I observed. Clearly, the whole thing was all for Candy. Aaron participated a bit, but truly my visits were more about making his wife happy. I have nothing but good things to say about both of them…in fact, they were some of the best clients I've ever had in my life. Candy was very sweet.

They really liked me too, and this arrangement might have gone on for some time. But I was in an ill-fated love affair at the time. I had fallen in love with a client, and decided it was time to pull myself off the market.

Falling in Love with Clients

I didn't mind letting any of my clients go, no matter how wonderful they were, because I had fallen in love. A hazard of the profession that I never thought could happen to me. Don was a big music executive, and I really fell for him, but it started out as just another night at work.

I met Don at the Beverly Hills Hotel Polo Lounge for a drink. We chatted; lightning certainly didn't strike. He was old, for one thing—well, at least to me, he was in his early fifties, but I was still in my twenties. He was a hard drinker, that I could see right away. He was very peremptory and bossy and what I thought of as "New York-Y"—one of those guys who was used to snapping his fingers while the world did his bidding. Very brash. And very rich—he had discovered a number of top musical groups and made millions. He was also in the middle of a punishing divorce with a vindictive wife.

I can't put my finger on what it was about this man that was so different. Looking back, I think what happened was that I became enmeshed in a relationship with an alcoholic, which had never happened to me before. The first few times I saw Don it meant nothing more to me than the $1,500 I got every time I saw him. But I really warmed to him; he was fun; being with him was all about the best restaurants, nightclubs, race-tracks, trips to Vegas. He wanted someone to drink with him, so I relaxed my rules and really started to enjoy cocktails. I also took up smoking cigarettes, just to keep him company. It was almost like dating a "bad boy" in high school. Partying hard was what he did; and I wanted to do whatever he did. I wanted to be cool, I wanted him to like me. And boy, did he like me.

We had a lot of fun, for awhile. But I fell in love. It was a classic co-dependent relationship; he was an alcoholic, and I was a call girl. I don't know why I thought we could make it, but for a good long time I certainly tried. About nine months into our relationship Don told me, "I'm falling in love with you; you can't do this anymore." I felt guilty about how much money he was spending—$1,500 a visit, three times a week—that added up fast. I was in love; I was crazy about him; this man was talking about us living together happily ever after. Eventually I stopped charging him and told him everything over a long drunken evening. My whole life story. Everything I had ever done and was still doing. Because I trusted him, and I loved him.

What a mistake. I learned a good lesson about keeping secrets. After that night things were never the same. He started pulling the whole "daddy" number on me, being the big powerful man who was going to save me from this tawdry life. In reality, I was trying to save *him* from drowning in alcohol. The relationship turned. It started slowly, insidiously, with remarks like, "You're gaining weight," "You're wearing *that?*" Degrading, rude comments meant to hurt me—the kind weak men make, because they take the easiest way to strike: at a woman's self-esteem.

I wasn't one to sit back and take it, either. "How dare you insult my body! Have you taken a look in the mirror lately, old man?" Neither of us were being kind or loving anymore. Don started picking on me for everything. I left my clothes and papers all over his house. I had too much makeup in his bathroom. He was renting a mansion in Beverly Hills furnished completely in white. There was never a speck of dust in the place. I got my period once and I'll never forget how he leaped out of bed to find the Spray-n-Wash at 5 in the morning. He hauled me out of bed to watch him huddle in the bathroom and fret over the sheets soaking in a tub of cold water. The honeymoon was over.

But I still loved him. I couldn't make myself leave him. I knew he wasn't the right person for me or good for me. But something in me insisted I could fix it, make him happy, that we could live happily ever after. I gave up, I surrendered to him; all I wanted to do was please him. He was a master controller and manipulator, and he played me. For the first year all I'd heard was "You are so wonderful. I love you just as you are; I respect all your choices." As we entered year two, I never heard anything like that again. And I had done what he wanted—I had quit the business.

I had given up all my clients and started a straight job in a real estate office. It was not fun to get such a tiny paycheck every two weeks, but I was absolutely committed to my new relationship and a "straight" life. I was doing the whole thing: living with Don, cooking, having a little office job, trying to get pregnant. But $1,800 a month after $1,800 a night was a shock, believe me. I didn't have time to miss the drama and excitement of being a call girl, because I had more than enough of that at home with the man who was supposed to love me.

Two years into our relationship we were living in an armed camp. All I heard about was my previous lifestyle, sly digs at my past, reproaches about my capacity to be faithful. I got grilled every time I came home from the supermarket! Bottom line: we could not get past my past. I had been the most wonderful thing to ever happen to him for the first year of our relationship. Now I was just a former prostitute he could never fully trust. No matter what I did, he would not let me forget it.

I loved Don with all my heart, but I finally had to leave him. Though I was devastated at the time that I couldn't conceive after more than a year of trying, it was probably all for the best. After months of terrible scenes and reconciliations, I packed my things and left Don's perfect white home for good. I started all over again, in a small Brentwood apartment. I had learned a couple of hard lessons. The first and most important: no more alcoholics. Never again. I had hardly been naïve about men, but he had drawn me into his twisted alcoholic mindset and games until I had almost lost my own mind. Which led to lesson number two: never give your power away to any man. I swore that I would never fall in love with a client again. It hurt way too much.

Going Pro

I took stock. I was thirty years old and my relationship hadn't worked out. I didn't have a husband or a baby. I had lots of disposable cash—I had squirreled some away before I moved in with Don—but it was time to take a hard look at the rest of my life. The easy money was just too tempting—I knew I was going back to being a call girl.

I decided that if that was truly going to be my life, it was going to be run like a business. I wasn't quite as sweet or accommodating as I had been. And I got a lot smarter about money. I had never gone crazy with cash—I was always frugal, and doing drugs is what made most girls lose all their money in a hurry. That was never a problem for me. I decided to take the next five years and make every bit of money I could.

I got back in touch with Madam Alex and started calling all my old clients. I tried to reach the Spellings, but after leaving a couple messages I let it go. There were plenty of others who were very glad to hear I was back. One of my first gigs after my two-year break was with a middle-aged banker. A very basic call—$1,200 was the fee. He wrote me a check, which I normally refused to take, but he was a banker, so I figured it was all right. Sure enough, a few days later the check bounced.

Before Don I would have just let this go. But this man had mentioned to me where he worked—at a private bank in Beverly Hills that serviced rich people only. I marched right into his office at the back of the building on Wilshire Boulevard and gave his secretary my name. I'm sure he had no idea who it was, but when he emerged from his office and saw me standing there, his face turned white.

"I believe we have some business, John," I said sweetly. "Shall we step into your office?" We got inside and John shut the door behind us. "You owe me $1,200," I said flatly. "And a check won't do this time. Please go get the cash." He did. I'm sure he never imagined a day like this would come.

I had made a promise to myself and meant to keep it: no more being taken advantage of, and no more falling in love. From now on, it was about me and my money.

George Lucas

I met George Lucas through a friend of mine, another call girl, in the Valley. George was one of her "regulars." It was quite ironic because though she had seen him many times, she had no idea what he did for a living. My girlfriend, Annie, called one day to ask me if I would do a double with her for a regular of hers named George. I said, "Fine, why not, I'll do it." Annie directed me to go to the Bel-Air Hotel the next night. "The suite's under the name 'Lucas' if you get lost," she added.

"*George Lucas*?" I asked.

"Yes, he's some kind of director, I think, or something."

I couldn't believe she didn't know who he was; this was just about the time the STAR WARS trilogy was being re-released and publicity was everywhere. The following evening I met Annie in the lobby and together we took the elevator to a suite and knocked. A sweet, sweet man opened the door. He was just a short little guy, but he radiated great energy. We were politely ushered in and led to a sofa in front of a blazing fireplace, where champagne sat chilling for us in a silver bucket. George was funny, kind, charming…just a wonderful personality.

We chatted for awhile and sipped champagne, talking about everything from love to relationships to the latest political scandal. My girlfriend had his number, so to speak, and had briefed me earlier on what he liked and didn't like. George preferred his evenings to start out like a classy date. I was charmed by his sweet, gentlemanly nature.

Finally Annie made a move and began to semi-seduce me on the couch. She started slowly taking off my clothes; I took off her clothes, and we started kissing and touching each other. It progressed into Annie going down on me, then I went down on her; the whole two-girl act. The three of us eventually all wound up in his king-size bed, where Annie climbed on top of him and rode him to a climax. That was the end of my first night with George Lucas.

There's a certain etiquette in the call girl business that clients must respect. George was a regular of Annie's; he saw her fairly frequently. She was extremely high-class, beautiful, and elegant, but every man likes variety. If a man wants to see a new girl, he has to get permission, on a certain level, from the girl who brought her to him. Many girls, of course, don't like new girls seeing their regular clients; others say fine, take her number. As we were preparing to leave George asked Annie if he could take my number, and she said "Sure." She was very secure in their long-term "relationship."

So George called me the next time he was in town from San Mateo, and I went to his suite alone. This second time we got into a very long, real conversation about family, and his kids, and so on. He didn't have a significant other at the time, and he was very committed to his children. We talked a bit about love again, and he wistfully mentioned a woman he had once dated and was still in love with. He would always love her, he told me. He never referred to her by name, but I was sure he was talking about to Linda Ronstadt, whom he had been romantically involved with years before and had apparently never gotten over.

He was such a nice man, I actually hoped that he would find an equally nice woman to marry. He called me a few more times…but I was afraid that in his mind he was starting to date me. The last time I saw him he started saying the same old lines I always heard from every long-term client, eventually: "You really shouldn't be doing this…what's a beautiful, smart woman like you *doing* this for?" I always wanted to retort: "What are *you* doing here with me?" Men can be so hypocritical…but this time, like always, I just said, "I know my reasons…what are yours?" My reasons were that I like to choose who I am with and how I will be treated; that I enjoy sex; and it has been very financially beneficial to me over the years. After that whole conversation, I never heard from George again.

A Beautiful Woman…with Bad Husbands

Jean-Claude Van Damme was another famous client I spent a great deal of time with. He and his then-wife Darcy, when they were still married. He was just gross—he hires men and women both. He loves anal sex—giving it and getting it. I used to have sex with Darcy; she did it to make him happy. Having sex with another woman disgusted her, but she did it for him. This was when she was obviously really trying to make her marriage work, before she divorced the movie star and went off with the Herbalife billionaire.

Jean-Claude would pay you well, but he'd fuck you like an asshole. He used to want me to watch him get fucked by men, which I found a little bizarre. I don't know if he is latently gay, or just exactly what his trip is, but the whole scene was just gross. He used to hire seven or eight girls at a time; and they'd all start making out with each other and using dildos on each other…just the full-on anything-goes act, the kind call girls hate to have to do, but knew we had to. Then the male prostitutes would come in and join in. There was nothing sensual or erotic about these scenes; I honestly think he enjoyed seeing his wife in demeaning, humiliating sexual situations. He would make these guys fuck her; the girls would have sex with her; we would all have to watch him getting fucked; it was a three-ring circus.

The man was simply a freak. Everyone of course, was all coked out during these binges, and I'm not a drug user. He used to want the girls to apply an ugly dark-brown lipstick before sex; then while he was fucking you, you constantly had to be smoking a cigarette—don't ask me why. I gave up smoking along with Don, so this was not a lot of fun.

The only thing I can say is that Van Damme paid well, which is the only reason anyone participated in this: $1,500 an hour, per person, which adds up quick. He's got issues. I used to leave there thinking, "Now, *that* really made me feel like a whore." And I know who I am, and I knew better than to be around that element of people, it was just gross. Here's the worst possible combination for a professional: sex, drugs, and gross people. All of which were in abundance at the Van Dammes. He is notorious in the business. Any number of girls—or guys— could tell you: he's pretty far out there.

Poor Darcy, she wasn't into it at all, and that was quite easy to see. I felt bad for her, because she was just doing it to make her husband happy. When they split and she married Mark Hughes, I was very happy for her. Now Mark was a really nice guy; he was supposed to be such a clean-living health fanatic. That was just bullshit. He got totally caught up in the hundreds of millions of dollars he was making. He did coke with Darcy; he drank; he took prescription drugs...I'm not sure where Herbalife and healthy living fit into *that* equation.

I stayed in touch with her...and actually did a *menage a trois* with she and Mark too. He wasn't that great a lover...again, Darcy was just trying to please her husband, doing a little act for him to spice things up. I'm not sure what it was with Darcy and these men...maybe it was just that these men were so rich and powerful and jaded that they needed this kind of "extra." She certainly could have done without it. But with Mark it was easy on my end...I was in and out in two hours, no problem. I'm sure they did it every other weekend or so, with one girl or another.

Look, karma is karma and it gets everybody eventually. Certainly I was shocked when Mark died suddenly and not happy about it, but I am happy that Darcy inherited a ton of his money. Believe me, she earned it. She paid some hard dues with those two husbands. I never hear from her anymore, which is a good sign. When that happens, you know that the girl is either completely out of the business or doing really well; and I hope she's living in a gorgeous house on a beach making love to beautiful 20-year-olds. She was a hot number; I hope she is finally enjoying herself and doing whatever she pleases.

Mrs. Robinson

Couples who bring another woman in to "spice things up" are a dime a dozen. Even Jane Fonda, in her recent autobiography that I read with great interest, confessed to participating in threesomes with prostitutes with one of her husbands to keep him happy. She is someone I view as strong, talented, intelligent, powerful...I would never have believed that she would do something like this, but she did it for Roger Vadim because she wanted to please him. I understand that whole concept, and also the idea of keeping the sexual heat high, the fires burning as it were, but a *menage a trois* could never make a marriage better.

Now maybe I'm just very straight in my real life, but I would never bring another woman into bed with me and a man I loved. I'm kind of a prude that way. I like women, but with a man that I really loved? I wouldn't dream of bringing another woman into that equation. It lowers your class level in a million ways. A man would never take you seriously after a scene like that if he was considering marrying you.

Mel Brooks and Anne Bancroft were the exception to the rule...I did a *menage a trois* with them and she actually enjoyed it more than he did, I'm sure. But they had a lifelong connection, a strong marriage.... This was quite recent, in fact less than a year before her sudden death. At the time both were well into their sixties, but certainly capable of still enjoying themselves. I know she did.

A girlfriend of mine lived a couple miles away from them, and Mel used to call her all the time. I joined her once on a call with him—it was no big deal. His wife certainly knew about it, it wasn't like we were doing anything behind her back. They called me several times after that by myself and I was happy to go. I would go to their house and they would bring out a bottle of champagne for me because I love champagne…and what Mel really wanted was for me to be with his wife. To please her.

It wasn't kinky or weird…I started out very sensually massaging her while he looked on, and he would wander in and out of the room. Finally he would go kiss her…I think he wanted to make his wife happy. Now, why they didn't invite a 20-year-old boy there, I don't know. But hey, look, they wanted to have fun…sex isn't an age thing. I think it's great that they still had the interest and excitement about their sex lives to even want to spice things up. Maybe just once a month they called a girl up. Many older women are very sexual creatures…she certainly was.

Every time I see him on TV I just say to myself, "Oh boy." If people only knew. These producers and their wives! But that's why I say, especially older men, when they get into their seventies they can get away with things.

New York, New York

The whole high-end call girl business in LA was over by the new millennium. All the madams were busted, jailed, out of business. It was time to change venues. I looked to the East Coast. I am a true California girl, born and raised, but I love the East. Men really love women there—real women. I was 35 years old at the time I decided to establish a presence in New York, no spring chicken, certainly not some skinny tan 20-year-old fresh off Zuma Beach. And I couldn't have been more popular.

An old friend in the business tipped me off to a very discreet facility in New York. The perfect place for the health-conscious, efficient, time-pressed man of the new millennium. Over the phone I made an appointment to see the woman who owned the business and we set up a job interview, more or less. I arrived at the address at 9:30am on the upper West Side of Manhattan, which was a perfectly normal big-city office building. I had on an Ann Taylor business suit and carried a good briefcase, and fit in perfectly with all the businesspeople walking the streets and crowding the lobby.

I got on the elevator and pressed 4. A young, good-looking guy, about 30, looking very sharp in a beautiful suit, was the only other passenger. He smiled at me and said, "Going to Tanya's?"

"Yes, this is my first time meeting her," I told him.

The elevator opened onto its own floor. It looked exactly like any mid-sized medical facility. Waiting room, magazines, receptionist in a white nurse outfit sitting at a front desk checking people in and out. The young man politely waited while I checked in with the receptionist. Another "nurse" stepped out from behind the desk and escorted me into the doctor's—madam's—office. She was on the phone but hung up and welcomed me graciously, her eyes quickly scanning me from head to toe, taking in every detail of my hair, outfit, and makeup in seconds. Obviously, she liked what she saw.

Tanya and I talked for a couple of minutes about the kind of business she ran. "We see businessmen here, who want to get in and get out, quickly, discreetly and safely. They book for an hour at a time, but it's doctor's hours—they pay $600 but get 40 minutes of the girl's time. They pay me, and you'll get $250. I have been running this business at this address for twelve years, and I am the best. You will never have to do anything you don't want to do here, and you will be treated well and professionally.

"You're beautiful and I know you'll do very well here. And,"— she smiled—"the man you were riding with on the elevator? He wants to see you. Right now."

I couldn't believe it. I wasn't at all prepared for this; I had thought this was just an interview. But what the hell, I was there, and I was there to make money. I was escorted to my own office. The funniest thing was how no one could ever imagine this was anything other than a doctor's office. My room had an examining table, x-ray equipment and arm pressure cuffs in the corner, swabs and wipes and needles in sterile jars on the stain-less-steel rolling table. Tanya smiled at my amazement and said, "Your client will be with you in ten minutes."

I looked around. There was a fluffy white bathrobe hanging in the tiny bathroom attached to the office. Lubricant and con-doms were stored in jars underneath the sink. I took off my clothes, wrapped myself in the robe and fifteen minutes later was having heated sex with the good-looking guy I had just met in the elevator. It was fast and furious, even though the setting could not have been more clinical. As the guy smiled and said, "See you next time," and walked out the door, I couldn't believe how easy this was. *I love New York!* I said to myself.

I was fascinated by the way this business ran. I saw three more clients that day and Tanya assured me that I would be busy for as long as I wanted to be. The whole arrangement was so brilliantly set up—I learned that many of her clients were high-profile guys who feared being followed by suspicious wives, business enemies, you name it. Anyone who followed a client into this appointment would see nothing but a doctor's office and a bunch of businessmen sitting around waiting for a blood test or something equally boring, no matter how far they got in. Clients were referral-only and thoroughly checked out before being allowed to make an appointment. Tanya ran a tight ship; as efficient as a Swiss watch.

There were two shifts—7am to 2pm, or 11am to 7pm, with the overlap for the always-busy executive lunch hour. I had to stay for the entire shift, booked or not. I happened to be very busy, because men always want to see the new girl, which I happened to be that week. I met some of the other women working there over the next few days and was very impressed. You would never guess they had sex for money. Some were young and beautiful, some were fortyish and had very pleasant nice-suburban-mom looks, but none of them looked like a hooker. It was a little strange, to be having sex on an examining table in a doctor's office, but it could not have been more smoothly run. "Clean-up nurses" came by every hour to change the table and sanitize the room after each client while I took a shower, leaving fresh white towels in the spotless bathroom for me.

I had to hand it to Tanya. That woman was a business genius. On the third or fourth day I idly started trying to figure out just how much money she must be making. At least 8 women there working at all times, 12 business hours a day, 200 clients a day, minimum, at $350 an hour after paying the girls. She was grossing at least $100,000 a day. New York rent is expensive, but still...and everyone who worked there was happy, too. It was safe, comfortable and lucrative.

But I'm a savvy businesswoman too. And there's only one reason someone like me would work at a place like that. And that's to build my client base in New York. It was against the rules, of course, but everyone did it: take clients' numbers and offer to see them privately. I didn't do it the first two times I worked in Tanya's office; I wanted to make a good impression on Tanya, in case I ever needed to work there again, but more importantly I wanted to take my time and find the right kind of clients for me. After I'd had several successful trips to New York, one of the men asked me for my private number. I was happy to give it to him.

The Big Spender

My biggest client, Roger, is a fabulously wealthy financier. He is worth billions, literally. Sixty years old, married to a society woman, three children, private jet, you name it. I could tell he really liked me the first time I saw him at Tanya's. He came back to see me every time I was in New York and eventually asked me for my number. He said, "I'd really like to see you in a more relaxed private setting. How would you feel about that?" I felt great about it. This was the kind of client I was looking to land.

I flew back to New York to see him a couple of times, and it soon became a permanent arrangement. Each month we stay in a suite at the Peninsula Hotel for 4 days/3 nights. Roger's very busy, of course, and always has business obligations during the daytime, even on Saturday and Sunday. So I fly in on a Friday, we get together for dinner at night, maybe see a play, then have sex and spend the night together Friday, Saturday and Sunday nights. I can do whatever I want during the days—he assumes

I'm shopping or at the spa. And that's what I did the first few times I made the trip.

This is a $20,000-a-month gig for one weekend a month in New York City. Let me stress that Roger is a multi-billionaire, so this isn't as outrageous as it may sound. That $20,000 a month is, to a man like Roger, like going out to dinner for a normal person. In fact, the other day I was musing that I really should charge him more because I'm not getting enough.

Roger is great, and I loved the job security. But a year or so into this arrangement I realized that I was not maximizing my time. There was plenty more money to be had in New York, and I did not want to miss out on it. I was there to work—and work is what I decided to do. $20,000 is not a lot of money…well, it's not enough for me. So I thought about the best way to make as much money as possible while I was there. I called all the numbers I had collected from working at Tanya's and set a schedule.

I rented my own suite at a small, discreet hotel around the corner and two blocks away from the Peninsula. I work out my schedule very carefully before I leave each month. I book four clients a day for Saturday, Sunday and Monday. I'm on my own all three days I'm in New York until 7pm, and it was crazy not to figure out the best way to incorporate more clients into my days. To make more money!

So, I wake up at the Peninsula and kiss Roger good-bye. He's always in a hurry to get going in the morning. I have a room-service breakfast and get dressed, then head over to my own hotel. I always dress conservatively, in a suit, and look like a businesswoman. The doormen at my hotel have never given me a second glance—they think I own an ad agency in L.A. and come see clients once a month. They're half-right, anyway. And it's here, in my own little suite running my own little business, that I like to believe I excel at providing what men want.

I create as luxurious an atmosphere as possible in my rooms. Beautiful linens, flowers, La Perla lingerie, candles burning, lots of ice and mixers for drinks, massage oil. I've have been doing this for a long time, and here's the thing about being a high-end call girl: It means being meticulous. I spend a lot of time and money on grooming. Bikini waxes are a must, as are blow-outs for my hair and perfect manicures and pedicures. It's a bit exhausting, seeing four clients in one day, and once I got a little tired of the excessive grooming. Instead of taking a full shower after one man left, I simply sponged off before the next client arrived. I regretted it the moment he got close to me. After we finished having sex, the man asked, "Did you see someone else this morning?" "Oh no, no, I've just been here waiting for you," I told him. But I was mortified. It was a real wake-up call. I had let my professional standards slide. Never again. After that, no matter what, I always took a full shower and shampoo between clients. I tip the maids extra to change my linens and service my room periodically throughout the day, and the hotel will even send someone up from the beauty parlor to fix my hair in my room if I have time.

All my regulars much prefer to visit me at my hotel rather than the "clinic." I don't feel bad about Tanya, because she has a never-ending supply of both workers and customers. And Roger, the guy I'm in New York to see? I feel two ways about him. On the one hand he is wonderful to me, generous and kind. He thinks that now that I have him in my life on a steady basis he's the only one I see. He's fallen into that mindset of preferring to forget how he met me. He treats me like a girl-friend, a mistress, someone he is just "helping out." We've been seeing each other for so long now maybe he really did forget!

I'm not a hooker in his mind, just a struggling businesswoman in L.A. he helps. He would be shocked if he knew I saw any other clients, much less while I was in New York on his dime. Every now and again I feel a slight pang of guilt. But the other, harder part of me says, "Screw him. He's got a wife and three kids and billions of dollars. I need to look out for myself!" So I do.

My business in New York has been consistent for five years. And all that money goes straight into a safety deposit box. I see four guys a day at $600 a pop, and put every cent of that $7,000-plus cash into one of my banks—I have many of them, in New York, California, the Bahamas. I don't buy clothes and shoes and crap. I save every penny. This is a business.

Voyeurs

I did have a client once, a very, very wealthy Arab in his eight-ies, who wanted to simply watch me have sex with another man. I don't think he was gay; more of a voyeur. I could not think of who in the world I could get to do this with me.... I was afraid to hire a male prostitute because I worried that they might have AIDS.

I asked one of my male friends, who was very open-minded, to come with me and explained what it was all about. He knew what I did for a living and had always been fascinated by it. I think he had a touch of gay in him...he certainly never came on to me in any way. But he was always completely into my stories about the whole scene...so I took a chance and made the proposition, making sure to tell him that we'd get paid. "Soo...would you be into it? "

He took a beat and then said, "Sure."

"Now look, just so we're clear, he's going to watch...he might touch you...he might touch me. I'm just not sure what is going to happen." But he was willing. The man just sat and watched us as we had very sensual sex. No touching, no talking, nothing. But we each got $1000 cash. He enjoyed the show.

That was the only time I've ever been with a *man* in front of another man. Another woman—all the time, that's standard. But hey, to each his own. This client, by the way, brings up another problem with clients I've encountered and in recent years has begun to take its toll on my business...these old guys are starting to die on me! Several men I see are completely geriatric, I'm talking seventies and eighties. I was talking with a girlfriend of mine about one of our old men, who's past participating but loves watching two girls together. We see him every now and then and were recently trying to set the best time to get together and visit him. I said, how about at the end of the month, because I'm going to New York next week. "I don't think we have a week...he could be dead by then!" And he really could. Fortunately no one has ever died while they're actually with me. That would be a little hard to explain.

by Olivia, Carly, Amanda, and Jennifer

But You Don't Look Like a Hooker

An incident with a client occurred the first time I ever worked at Tanya's place in New York that has stuck in my mind for a long time. Apparently one of the clients had seen me while he was there for an appointment with another woman. Tanya called me after I returned home to L.A. saying, "You have to let me know when you're coming back... there's a man who's dying to meet you."

I didn't give it much thought until my second trip to New York, where my very first appointment was with this kindly, sixty-something retired clothing manufacturer from New Jersey. "This guy's been calling and calling, asking when you'd be here again," Tanya told me that morning when I arrived. "You really made quite an impression on him."

When Len walked in the door he grabbed my hand and stared into my face. "You're back! I can't believe it! I've been think-ing of you all month, ever since I saw you here last time! What is your story? You can't be a professional, you look like some rich man's wife from the suburbs! You're the girl next door, all grown up!

Len was really perturbed. Someone who looked like me could not, in his mind, sell sex for money. I launched into a sad story. "Len, I live in San Francisco and have been married for a long time. My husband is rich, but we don't have sex anymore; it's more of a business relationship at this point. He has a mistress; he hasn't touched me for years, and I have needs. So I decid-ed to come to Tanya's last month on a whim. Just to let off steam. I've never done anything like that before...but I had to do something. I need to be touched again." My *Desperate Housewife* speech.

Len bought that story hook, line and sinker. That kind of situation he understood. He certainly also enjoyed the sex that followed. It was OK now, because really I was a "nice" woman. Someone he was helping out. After my ill-fated affair with Don, I was never completely honest with another man again. It's all right to tell a client that you accepted a job because you were desperate, or lonely, or had an emergency where you had to put your hands on some cash immediately. That they can justify in their own minds. But a woman who sells sex full time, as a real honest-to-God business? That's a line they don't want to cross. A professional prostitute is not who men are looking to sleep with.

Len left our session smiling and happy. "I knew you couldn't be really be a prostitute; you just don't have that look," he said and went on his way, back to his wife and retirement in Saddle River. If I was honest, or wanted to get into it, I would have said, something like, Len, wake up. Call girls don't look any certain way. You have no idea when you're sitting in a restaurant or at a party or even at a business meeting which women around you are willing to provide sex for money. There are a lot of us, and 99% of people have no idea and would never guess. We're your next-door neighbor, your friend from the dog park, the woman you chat with at the nail salon. People have no idea. Men are bad enough—but other women tend to be the most judgmental about the subject.

I have a girlfriend I've known for almost fifteen years, and we're close enough that she knows what I do for a living. She's made it very clear over the years that she doesn't understand how I could do something like that...she's very strait-laced. I've always felt a wave of disapproval coming from her when the subject of my business came up. Donna is smart, and pretty, but nothing ever seemed to really come together for her.

I watched her life unfold as we've both gotten older. She's now in her late thirties, endured a series of office jobs that were tedious and low-paying as she searched for Mr. Right. Somehow, he never came along. I met some of her boyfriends, and I certainly wouldn't have slept with them for love alone. A year or so ago she got laid off from her job. She was really desperate for money; she didn't know how she was going to pay her rent. When I made her a proposition, she was ready to listen.

"Listen, Donna, I will send you to the easiest client I have. He's a little old man in the Valley, sweet as can be. All he wants is a massage—you don't even have to take off your clothes! It's easy money, I promise." Under any other circumstances, she wouldn't have even listened to this, but I could tell she was wavering. Finally, she said, "OK, set it up."

She called me that Friday morning, freaking out, saying she couldn't go through with it. I was very patient. I said "Listen, Donna, I will go if you really can't bring yourself to do this, but I am trying to help you. You're the one who keeps crying to me about money..." "All right, all right, I'll do it!" she said, and hung up abruptly.

Two hours later Donna was on my doorstep with a big smile on her face. She waved $500 cash at me and said, "You weren't kidding. That was the easiest money I ever made. That was *ridiculously* easy." She was happy, and in fact has gone back to see him a couple of times. I'm happy to have made the introduction — my intentions were truly to help a friend through a rough patch. Lately, Donna's even started dropping hints about being ready to meet other clients of mine. The easy money...I'll say it again, it's an addiction as bad as crack, and anyone can get hooked. *Anyone.*

My attitude is don't judge, and don't think you can tell a call girl just by her looks. The general American public has no idea about what truly goes on in this world.

You're Such a Nice Girl....

One of my clients, a businessman I met in New York, made enough money on Wall Street to retire to his home state of Kentucky and live on a beautiful estate in the heart of horse country. I go to see him every two or three months. He's a sweetheart. I stay in a beautiful inn way out in the sticks and he sneaks away for the weekend to see me. Of course he's been married for about 30 years. He gets so excited when I'm coming... he calls me two and three times a day for a couple of weeks leading up to my visit. "I can't wait to see you...." "I miss you..." "There's no one like you...."

Talk like that simply annoys me at this point in my life. I don't need to hear it and I don't have time for it. The ten-thousand-dollar check I get for three days work—not hard work, mind you, this guy is actually good in bed—is what I'm after. The last time I was in Kentucky I really tried to do nice things for him...massages, wine, lingerie. He's a good customer, after all, and I want to keep him happy. It was time to show a good account how much their business was appreciated. But it might have worked too well. I was so nice to him that he started to feel guilty, saying things like, "I don't do enough for you...I can't give you what you really need..." The very last thing I want is for him to leave his wife. I'm not looking to get married. I don't want our situation to change...at all!

But if you see them long enough men cast you in their minds as the "other woman." I've been the other woman, for real, before. I've heard that whole, "I'm going to leave my wife for you." I was a bit younger and more naïve then. Now, I don't want anyone leaving anyone. I don't want to be their girlfriend or their wife. I want to be their daytime lover—who gets paid.

Here's the good thing about 95% of my clients: they have a lot to lose, and I like it that way. They are married, rich and conservative. They do not want a scandal and they do not want a divorce. Prostitution, for me, has become a daytime business, because most men are married. They go home to their wives and kids at night. Because I work with married men, their nights are spoken for. It works for me, because I like to be home at 6pm too. Nighttime is where the drugs and alcohol start to come in, and I don't like that stuff. Been there, done that...I don't want fun, I don't want clients falling in love with me. I want my business to run smoothly.

Making Love to Women

I like having sex, all kinds of sex. It doesn't faze me in the slightest to have sex with a woman. I consider myself heterosexual, but the idea of bisexuality intrigues me. When I was very young, 18 years old, I actually had sex with a girlfriend and her boyfriend. Not for money of course, we were all just young and wild and curious. I didn't know what I was doing, or how to please either one of them, but I've certainly always been very sexually open.

In my work life, I like women. In fact, I love doing scenes with other women. On a sexual level they're much better then men, for the most part, though a big part of me remains attracted to the alpha male. I'm a woman, and a very primal part of me will always be turned on by men—that's just chemistry.

Maybe there's a part of me that's afraid I might like sex with women too much! I have one female client, a married woman who books appointments and comes to see me by herself. I met her through a friend of mine—not a call girl—in my "real life" as it were. We really liked each other, eventually I told her what I did for a living, and she made an appointment! She misses feeling in love, feeling adored, the excitement and passion of a romance. That's been gone from her marriage for years. She's 50, her husband's 55 and no doubt has a mistress or two. Her husband made his money in oil, and they live on Fifth Avenue, but there's no passion or love there. She told me, "I never thought I could feel this way again. But I met you."

And here's the funny thing: I love her. We are girlfriends, first and foremost. We always have dinner together first at a great restaurant. She was clearly physically attracted to me right from the start, and the funny thing is that my attraction to her is growing. As my only woman client, she is the only person I ever have to think beforehand about what I'm going to say or do. I don't dress up for men—that is, outside of the bedroom—but for her, I put a lot of thought into my outfit. She's the only client whose opinion I truly care about. We have such a great time together. She always says to me as I'm leaving: "You have made my whole month. This is the best way I can possibly imagine to spend my husband's money." And it's quite a lot of his money— $1500 every time I see her. She books me for four hours. But the truth is, I like her so much I'd do it for less— something I'd never do for a man—even though I've never told her so.

I asked her, flat out, once, "Are you gay?" And she said no. "I just want to feel *something* again. I need to feel alive." In her mind having sex with another man would be being unfaithful, but another woman doesn't count. Though I enjoy being with them, I tend to fake it a lot with other professional women in my work life. We're generally there just to put on a show for a man. This woman is a whole different level of feeling. I find myself with butterflies in my stomach before we meet. I feel a bit nervous and shy and anxious to please, as if we're on a real date. There is no man client in the world who makes me nervous. It's funny; I guess I have a crush on her; I like her more every time I see her.

Who knows, maybe I really am gay. It's hard to say after twenty years in this business; I've been doing what other people want me to do and being who they want me to be for so long that my own true desires have gotten lost. I couldn't actually say if I'm gay or not, because I honestly don't know what my heart, or body, truly desires.

What Men Want

I'm sensual, kind and loving. I'm also a very good, practiced lover. If you're a client of mine you are certainly going to get fucked, that's a given—but I have to say that most of my clients want more than that. They want a new experience. They want some passion and excitement and a bit of an illicit thrill. These are high-powered businessmen, very rich and respectable, but pent-up. These are good-looking Wall Street guys in tailor-made 3-piece suits with money to burn. They can have anything they want.

They want to have fantastic great sex with a beautiful woman, and I deliver that. What surprises me is that probably almost half of my clients in New York are in their late twenties and thirties. It's so ironic—being a good call girl has nothing to do with age. Every time I go back to New York, I wonder.... Are they going to call me back? And every time they do. In fact, at age 40, I'm bombarded with calls! When are you coming? I can't wait to see you!

These young guys, in their early thirties...handsome, designer suits, buff and well-groomed, great bodies, they smell good... but most of them are married. Those few who are single? Sure, they probably have a nice girlfriend named Molly who's a kindergarten teacher. And yes, they love Molly, but sometimes they want something a little different. And this is something they can walk right over to do on their lunch hour. They can take Molly out that night. The married ones are home on the 5:20 commuter train and no one is the wiser.

My younger clients remind me once again that it's not all about looks. It's about what you give to a human being. Because most hookers don't give anything of themselves. Yes, they'll suck your dick or let you have mechanical sex with them, but it's very cold. 90% won't kiss you. They say, "OK, you've got 45 minutes, let's get to it." They keep one eye on their watch the whole time, pushing you out the door, just getting it done so they can have the money. I've never been like that. Well, not with anyone I like, and I like all of my regular New York clients.

I love to kiss and cuddle and give massages! I am a sensual creature and I try to make love to every one of my clients. That's what it's all about at the high end of this business: to provide a sensual, loving experience. Most women who've been in this business a long time have completely deadened their whole sense of fun and even sexuality. There's a big difference between fucking and making love. A man knows when he's just fucking someone who's lying there just going through the motions. I never do it. Bottom line: If I was a man, I'd go to me!

It almost makes me sad, how many of my clients say, "Oh my God you are the most incredible lover I've ever had…there's no one like you…no one's ever done these things to me before…" I have to wonder where they've been and who they've been with. I guess I should be glad they're so deprived—it's good for business.

For the most part I see only regular clients now. People with whom I've established a real relationship. The men love the comfort zone of being with somebody they can trust and know something about. They tell me about their business problems, their kids, you name it. They aren't looking for a blow-job or a quick fuck from a 20-year-old with the most fantastic body. I offer something they can't: a real discussion. All most men are looking for is some kind of *connection*.

This hit home for me about ten years ago when I was with one of my regular clients. We were rolling around on the bed and I was doing my whole number: "Ohhhh…fuck me fuck me fuck me..." And Jonathan said, "Amanda, stop. I just want to make love to you." I was so embarrassed. I stopped all my frantic moving around and vocals and just made love to him. It was a wonderful experience. And as we were lying together afterwards Jonathan said in a tired voice, "Amanda, I didn't want to fuck you today. I wanted to have an experience. I haven't had any kind of romantic encounter with my wife for five years. I don't want to fuck you. I wanted to touch you, to reach you, to feel that you wanted me."

This was a great lesson to me and a real turning point in my business. I'm not saying there aren't men who just want to get off. There are plenty of them out there, and I saw plenty of them while I was in my twenties. But I've established my business with men who are looking for a bit more of a real interpersonal connection. You don't keep clients for seven and ten years on the basis of fucking alone. I keep clients based on giving them something they miss from their life or maybe never had. Whether that's excitement or intimacy or sex games...as corny as it may sound, I really provide them sexual healing.

Money Money Money

Literally, I won't be physically able to do this job for much longer. But I've made enough money so I won't have to. My mindset is starting to change. I'm starting more and more to look to a future beyond this business. Which is very hard to do. It's the whole concept of, "Oh, I'll do this the smart way and be out of the business in ten years." You can't do it. It's so easy to get in and so hard to get out. You make $500 an hour for a few years—tax free, I might add—and then you start looking for a job? A job that might pay $15 an hour before taxes? Come on. You can see how hard it would be. I saw for myself how hard it was!

This business has been very, very good to me financially. My goal for retirement is a net worth $4 million, and I'm almost there. I hope to reach my goal by the age of 42, then go off and figure out what it is I really want out of life for myself. Thank you men, for the money. I plan to laugh all the way to the bank.

A client of mine, a top accountant, is obviously aware of what I do for a living. For the past ten years he has helped me with some of my money—turning piles of cash into solid investments. I've been smart. I have a substantial amount of money saved apart from my various investments. I have $1.5 million in cash in safety deposit boxes all over the United States.

I've let the accountant into my financial life to a certain extent, but a bigger part of me doesn't trust banks and certainly doesn't trust the IRS. In my twenties I was young and foolish and used to buy $500 shoes and designer dresses. But when I turned 30 I got smart. For the past ten years I've shopped at the Gap and Banana Republic and Ann Taylor. I wear very basic clothes to see clients. Black and white. Classic pieces, well-made, good labels, but nothing fancy. Forget Manolo Blahnik and all that crap. Some of my super-rich clients have glanced at my shoes disapprovingly once or twice, but you know what? Tough shit. I'm willing to spend a lot of money on fancy lingerie—it's good for business—but I won't waste money on something like clothes. I've seen far too many girls who had great closets of clothes and more shoes than Carrie Bradshaw but couldn't pay their rent or buy a car.

I have traveled all over the world on business. London, Spain, Ibiza, Paris, Austria, Germany, Italy, Greece.... I went with a client to Sarajevo, for God's sake! No one believes me when I say that I've actually been to Sarajevo, but I have. On business. The traveling has been fun, but honestly, I'm just like any other business traveler now. I'm sick of the plane rides and jet lag. It gets wearing. It takes energy to get off a plane looking great and being excited and acting happy to see the client. Sometimes, after a bumpy flight and crowded airport, I don't want to be nice. I'm *not* excited to see my client. But that's the downside for anyone who travels all the time for business. My adventurous spirit hasn't gone completely; I still enjoy jumping on a plane to an unknown destination.

My life right now is planning for the next phase of my life, and my clients' money is funding my future. I'm not spending any of that to live up to any certain image. Business is booming, I'm doing fine looking and dressing the way I always have. It's all about what works and is comfortable for me, because I don't want to work for more than two more years. When I get out I will be financially secure. I own my house in Los Angeles, I paid cash for my new SUV—if there is one thing I feel strongly about, it's that I will not become a casualty of this business.

My accountant tells me I could stop right now—and he doesn't even know about all my cash salted away all over the country! But something holds me back and keeps me working. After I have a tough day with a difficult client, I swear I'm getting out, and I mean it, for a few hours at least. Unfortunately this business is in my blood. The money is addictive, and I'm hooked. Bottom line? At age 40 I'm still not ready to count my cards and call it a day.

Jennifer Young

Hollywood Princess

My father was Gig Young, a tall, good-looking actor who was nominated three times for an Academy Award, finally winning for 1969's *They Shoot Horses, Don't They?* His career went strong from the forties to the seventies and he appeared in more than 70 films, including *The Music Man*, *Kid Galahad* (with Elvis Presley), the original *Three Musketeers*, *Teacher's Pet* (with Doris Day and Clark Gable), and *Young at Heart* (with Frank Sinatra). He was very much entrenched in old Hollywood, and even his name, our name, has an interesting cinematic twist to it. My father's real name was Byron Barr, but early in his career (1942) he played a character named Gig Young in *The Gay Sisters*, with Barbara Stanwyck. Women went crazy for the name—Gig really stuck in everyone's minds, so he legally changed it. He was officially Gig Young from that point on.

My father was a real character. Everyone who knew him loved him; people still get excited when I tell them who I am. But he had a dark side to him, a very dark side. He was married five times, became an alcoholic who abandoned me, and finally killed himself and his last wife.

So much for Hollywood royalty.

My mother, Elaine Young, was my dad's fourth wife. He was married to the actress Elizabeth Montgomery of *Bewitched* fame for about four years. When they separated, he was shown a house by a real estate agent in Beverly Hills. That real estate agent was my mom, Elaine. They fell in love, he got divorced, they were married, and a year later I appeared.

Unfortunately, my father was an alcoholic. A bad one. The first year my parents were married my mother convinced him to go to AA, so he stayed sober, but only for that first year. Hollywood is not the place to be if you want to stay on the wagon, because everywhere my father went, people tried to get him to drink, to "loosen him up" because it made him "more fun" to be with. Well, it worked. It just wasn't all that much fun for my mom. She became more and more unhappy as his drinking spiraled out of control.

When I was just three years old, my father slapped my mother across the face in a drunken fury. They struggled and I fell down a flight of stairs. That was the last straw for my mother. She packed us up and we left my father.

On the way out, he warned my mother that if she left, he would never see me again. He thought he could make her stay by threatening me with abandonment, because he knew how much my mother loved me and would want me to see my father. But she really did want what was best for me—she wanted me to be safe and protected. We left, and my dad kept his promise. I never saw him again unless it was at the movies or on TV.

I spent many years of my life trying to understand why he left me when I was such an adorable little kid. But he was an alcoholic, and one thing I learned was that his leaving was not about me, it was about him. That was a long, hard lesson to learn, let me tell you.

The best present my mother ever gave me was putting me in therapy at the age of six. It was very difficult, but it helped a lot in the long run. When I was about 10 or 11 years old I went searching for my father, because I found out where he lived. I took one of my girlfriends with me. We pretended to sell Girl Scout cookies, and managed to get into the apartment building. My girlfriend went one way; I went another. I got right up to the door to knock, but couldn't do it because I was petrified. I was so afraid he might yell at me. I didn't know what I would say when he saw me. What would he do? Would he reject me again? I just couldn't make myself knock on that door; I went home instead. To this day I regret that I didn't work up the courage to just knock.

Realtor to the Stars

After my dad left, my mother had to be both parents to me. She did receive a very small amount of child support until the time he killed himself, but it was minimal, so it was up to her to support us. She chose real estate and worked very hard to build a career for herself. At first she worked for Mike Silverman, who was one of the biggest names in real estate in Beverly Hills in the 1970s. He was a movie star-handsome bachelor who was good at his business, but tough to work for. My mom used to come home and cry almost every night.

Eventually she had enough and formed her own real estate business—and she was very, very good at it. I was always very proud of what she accomplished. Her clients included Elvis Presley, Elizabeth Taylor, Warren Beatty, Burt Reynolds, Frank Sinatra, Barbra Streisand, Stevie Wonder, Cher, M.C. Hammer, David Geffen, and President John F. Kennedy. She even handled the now infamous O.J. Simpson estate on Rockingham and once sold a $25 million property belonging to the Sultan of Brunei. More recently her listings included Smokey Robinson's multimillion-dollar estate.

Mom had a lot of chutzpah. When she listed her first million-dollar home in the 1970s, her client pointed out that the place only had one bathroom.

"Well, what do you expect for a million dollars?" she asked. She put that anecdote into the book she wrote, *A Million Dollars Down*. Mom always said that the secret to her success was in keeping tabs on the personal lives of celebrities. If she heard that a famous couple were divorcing or marrying, she figured they would be selling or buying a home, so she would contact them. And she would drive them to see properties in a Rolls-Royce convertible with the license plate "Elaine 7." She really was a hot ticket.

My mother was a searcher, though. And what she was searching for was the perfect man. She married six times; the average length of each union was about four years. After my dad the movie star came the songwriter and composer Jule Styne's son Stanley, followed by Sal Vilacchi from Chicago. Sal was an Italian-mobster kind of guy, but I really did like him. Then there was Jonathan, the husband I didn't like or respect at all. He borrowed money from my mother and then got her into a business scheme that almost bankrupted her.

After Jonathan my mother married William Levey, who was also involved in the movie business. I was being a really rebellious teen at the time so we didn't get along at first—we eventually became the best of friends. He took me everywhere and was proud to say I was his stepdaughter. He was a writer, producer, and editor, though his movies had titles like *The Happy Hooker Goes to Washington* and *Skatetown, USA*—Dorothy Stratten's first film appearance. He also put Debra Winger in her first movie. He gave me a bit part in my first movie, *Lightning, The White Stallion*, which starred Mickey Rooney and Susan George—and that, I have to admit, was a great experience. To this day Bill is the closest thing to a father I ever had; I consider him my family.

Tanya Roberts Was No Angel

My mother was always a lot of fun, and because of her business she knew everyone in Hollywood and Beverly Hills. While I was growing up she used to throw the most raging parties. One of them was especially memorable because of Tanya Roberts. She was one of *Charlie's Angels* and much later on appeared on *That '70s Show*. She came over to one of my mom's parties; a friend brought her along as a guest. I remember her being completely wasted, high out of her mind, and stripping in front of 13-year-olds.

I'll never forget it. One night this gorgeous girl just wandered right into my bedroom. She was breathtaking, beyond beautiful. I was hanging out in my room with my little boyfriend and some of our friends; we were all about 13 or 14. She waltzed in and started taking off her clothes, doing a little striptease for a bunch of middle schoolers. I think she must have been on Quaaludes. My friends and I couldn't believe our eyes.

A friend of my mom's walked by and saw what was happening, so she went to inform my mother, "Tanya Roberts is in your daughter's room doing a striptease act. She's lifting up her skirt and she doesn't have any underwear on."

Meanwhile Tanya was grabbing the asses of everyone in sight. Then she plopped down heavily on my bed. She lifted her top—she was braless, as well—and slurred, "Come here, honey." She grabbed me and threw me down, and I had no idea what she was going to do next. All I could think was… "Whoa!"

My mom burst in on Tanya Roberts and me grappling on the bed while all the boys were pointing and laughing. We were just kids; we thought the whole thing was funny. My mom was unamused. She grabbed Tanya off the bed by her arm and pulled her into the living room, where she started yelling at her at the top of her lungs. Tanya just stood there, swaying, saying things like, "It's okay, man. Just chill; don't worry."

My mother was furious—she wasn't about to chill, but Tanya was so fucked up I doubt any of this was even registering. Finally she started to yell back at my mother, and the two of them really had it out, right there in the living room. The scene ended with Tanya being thrown, literally, right out the front door.

Life was never dull at our house.

A Shocking Death

After my parents divorced, my father, unlike my mother, did not remarry for another decade. He met his fifth wife, Kim Schmidt, on the set of a movie he was doing with Bruce Lee, *The Game of Death*. That title was certainly portentous, because

Bruce Lee died during filming and then my father's relationship with Kim turned violent and explosive. In angry moments she would taunt him, telling my father that his career was over and that he was no good in bed. From what I understand he was drinking more and more and their fights became uglier and more violent every day. Then one night, during one of their fights, he shot her and then turned the gun on himself. They had only been married about three weeks. The New York City police found the Oscar he had won for playing a dance-marathon barker in *They Shoot Horses, Don't They?* beside their bodies.

I was in high school when my father shot himself. I opened the door of my house after school and found myself surrounded by paparazzi that were flashing cameras and shouting intrusive questions. I didn't know what was happening, so I called my mother at work. She gently explained that my father had died.

Of course, it was all over the media that night. It was huge news, on top of the hour, every hour for a couple of days. Can you imagine watching stories about your father's death on the evening news? It was horrific; I cried myself to sleep that night. And my poor mother was crushed; she was sad for months—she and my father had remained in touch by phone and letters.

Even after all these years it is still hard to believe that my father, my own father, killed someone and then killed himself. No one really knows what happened, but I believe it was an accident. I believe he accidentally shot his new wife and then, overcome with guilt and remorse, killed himself. Whatever really happened, no one should have to remember their father that way.

by Olivia, Carly, Amanda, and Jennifer

Beverly Hills Brat

Just like army brats have their own set of peculiarities, so do celebrity kids with famous parents. At Beverly Hills High, where I went to school, drugs were plentiful. So were nose jobs, fancy cars and parties. Tobacco, alcohol, pot, and Quaaludes were all over the place. Many kids, me included, often took brief campus breaks to get high between classes.

Learning was never my main interest. Boys and parties, or parties and boys—now that was another story. And I was a real entrepreneur. With a friend of mine, David—who sadly died of a drug overdose after we graduated—I used to throw huge parties in million-dollar estates, and charge admission at the door. The booze and drugs were always flowing at these events. I really don't know how we got away with it, because the crowds sometimes got really rough. At one party a fight broke out and some poor guy went flying through a plate glass window. At another I was shocked to see a good friend from elementary school carted away in an ambulance after she overdosed. She almost died, which cooled my jets for a couple of weeks, but not much longer.

In many ways I was a typical teenager—too involved with boys and friends, not involved enough with school. It's just that I lived in a really privileged place with a lot of people who lived, and still live, larger than normal lives, so everything was always overblown and overdone. I'm not complaining, mind you, but I also would never consider it a normal place to grow up. My high school life was anything but normal. Everyone thinks when you grow up rich in Beverly Hills you have no problems—I think I actually had more problems!

Nicolas Cage—a bit of a nerd back then—asked me to his prom. I *went* to the prom with Michael Landon, Jr., who was absolutely great-looking and who I had a crush on that year. My long-time high school boyfriend Mark was best friends with Nicollette Sheridan's high school boyfriend, and the two of us were great girlfriends for a couple of years. We had sleep-overs all the time and hung out constantly. Her fling-turned-main squeeze Leif Garrett was the first person to ever offer me a line of cocaine. I turned it down, which was ironic, because I would certainly run into problems with that drug a couple of years down the road. At the time I wasn't tempted; I just said, "Naah, but I'll take a half of Quaalude instead."

Celebrity offspring were everywhere during high school. Victoria Sellers was another great friend of mine. She owned the first BMW convertible at Beverly Hills High School. The license plate said "I KNOW," because she got so sick and tired of people coming up to her and telling her how hot her car was. She was a punk rocker kind of chick, and I loved hanging out with her. Because we both had famous fathers that had died too young—Peter Sellers and Gig Young—we felt a common bond.

Leif, Nicollette and I used to hang out at Farrah Fawcett and Ryan O'Neal's Malibu beach house all the time in high school. Griffin O'Neal was incorrigible; he was constantly battling his hot-tempered father. Tatum had quite an attitude—as befits the youngest Oscar winner ever. Ryan O'Neal was the first adult man to turn me on to marijuana. One day we were hanging out at the house, and he rolled a big fat joint for my girlfriend and me. We sat in his bedroom under a huge oil painting of Farrah Fawcett and got high.

I loved high school and all my friends…it seemed the fun would never end. When we graduated, the party continued. But I knew what I wanted to be: a singer.

The Playboy Mansion

Growing up in Beverly Hills there was no way to escape cocaine. It was inevitable that you would run across it, and the peer pressure to do drugs was intense. If you didn't do drugs, you weren't in the "in" crowd, and I wanted to fit in and be cool. It wasn't long before I was into cocaine, just like all my friends.

Liza Greer was definitely a cool person. She and I had been friendly in high school. Years later she would become infamous for being a high-class call girl, but back in those days she was undeniably the most beautiful girl at Beverly Hills High. I was a little intimidated by her, because she was older than I was and so gorgeous that the boys would line up in the hallway just to watch her walk by. Breathtaking does not begin to describe it.

Liza had a hard life; her upbringing wasn't ideal. She was passed around a lot and got into sex and partying at a very young age. She was a regular at the Playboy Mansion, and as soon as I got out of high school she started taking me with her. We used to tan nude in the tanning beds by the grotto. I'd watch the monkeys swing from the trees and the pink flamingos wander the grounds while being waited on by staff.

Hugh Hefner was the most incredible host; he threw amazing parties. He is the only person in the world I can imagine commanding hundreds of guests at a party to stop eating, drinking, flirting—whatever they were doing—because it was time to watch a movie. And everyone would obey! He always had the new movies before they came out in the theaters. Once or twice I got to sit next to him during the film, which was very cool.

I always admired Hugh Hefner for being such a pioneer and giving the world such a great release! I had such good times at his Mansion, and actually had a photo shoot at the private home of Playboy's wonderful photographer Richard Fegeley. He took some gorgeous pictures of me and there was some talk about me appearing in *Playboy*, but my mother absolutely put her foot down. "Not as long as you live with me!" she told me. She was so upset that I didn't pursue it, but it's always been my dream to pose for Playboy, the most awesome publication in the world. I would do it today in a heartbeat.

James Wilder

At one point I was between boyfriends and my mother fixed me up with James Wilder. Now remember, my mother always knew everyone in town because she sold them their houses.

We went out a couple of times. We would sit at Chin-Chins and literally not say a word to each other—I don't know why. And then we'd go back to his house and fool around. We dated sporadically on and off for six months, and then we didn't talk for awhile.

James called me after we had stopped seeing each other for a month or two, and I wanted to see him. He invited me up to his house, and I was happy to go. I could tell he was high when I got there, but everything seemed all right. After a little while we started kissing. Then he threw me down on his bed and got very forceful. I didn't like the way it was going. I kept saying, "Please stop, you're hurting me. Please, please stop. Stop, stop, stop!"

But he wouldn't stop. Even though he was really hurting me, I finally stopped protesting and struggling and just stared out the window until he was finished. And then I grabbed my clothes and got out of there as fast as I could. I just ran.

I was in tears. I was so swollen down there it looked like a couple of balloons. I remember coming home and pouring ice in the bathtub. I couldn't get the water cold enough. I sat in ice baths for three days, crying.

A few weeks after the forced sex James called with some lame excuse for me to come up to his house, like I'd left a shirt there. He made a point of telling me a buddy of his was in town. The buddy was some big football star. James said, "Why don't you come over and pick it up. I want to see you and say 'hi.'"

I was thinking he was just nervous and feeling me out to see if I was going to tell on him. At the time I figured that since I'd had sex with him before, even though that one particular time I hadn't been willing, what was I going to do about it? People talk about things like this more openly now, but I really don't know how often any woman is believed if they've willingly had sex with the person before.

I did go up to see him though. I was still quite upset and certainly not as nice as I usually am. In fact I had a little bit of an attitude. I was thinking to myself, "Am I out of my frickin' mind? Even though it's daytime, here he is at home with some huge football guy."

His friend was really large physically, and I don't think there was a housekeeper or anyone else there in the house. After I got there I was thinking, "Great. Now they'll both get me." I was very edgy and I didn't stay long; I wanted to get the hell out of there. James was being very, very nice to me, but just being in his house again made me nervous.

Deep down, I know why I went up there. All I wanted was an apology. Something. Anything. I just wanted him to sit down and say, "I know I was pretty rough with you. I know you were crying. I'm sorry."

Because I never got that apology I have always been very hurt about that whole incident. I used to see James around town sometimes and noticed that he stared at me. I wonder if James even remembers what happened. Do guys remember things like that?

For a long, long time I was embarrassed to even talk about this, because I'd willingly had sex with him before, but when you say "no," it means fucking "no!" And he certainly must have known he was hurting me. I wasn't very happy about it, but I never told on him. Till now, anyway.

Heidi Fleiss Before She Was Heidi Fleiss

I had an intense friendship for a decade with the girl who would become infamous worldwide. But it started as just another night out. A couple of years after I graduated from high school,

I was introduced to Heidi Fleiss by a guy named Russell Evans at a nightclub. The two of us immediately hit it off. Soon we were partying buddies, then best friends. Inseparable. Heidi and I literally slept in the same bed for years, until we actually became roommates and each had our own room. I was always aware, right from the start, that Heidi had a little crush on me. Her brother used to tease her about it, saying, "Why don't you just tell Jen that you've got a crush on her?" She'd say, "Shut up, Jesse!" and push him away.

I'll never forget one night when it was pouring rain and she showed up at my new apartment in West Hollywood. I was 22, and I'd just moved out of my mom's house into my first place, and the cable was out due to the torrential downpour. I had been sitting around really bored, so I was thrilled to see her. I said, "I'm so glad that you're here! There's no TV, and all I have is the movie *Roxanne* on video!" Heidi looked a little out of it. "Well, I've got *this*!" she said, and dumped a huge bunch of blow on a mirror. She looked pretty wasted and was literally falling asleep; she was clearly drugged out and exhausted. I just did a little line, while she did a huge line. Next thing I knew she was passed out in my bed. I couldn't believe such a huge line didn't keep her awake, but she was out like a light. I must have rewound and watched "Roxanne" at least 10 times that night.

Heidi worked odd jobs in those days, and I think her dad helped her out a bit financially. When we first met, she worked at Cravings Restaurant as a waitress. I used to pick her up after she'd get off work, and she'd grab some food and a couple bottles of wine. Then she'd come to my place we'd hang out, eating, drinking, and laughing.

Back in those early days Heidi wanted to be just like my mother, a hotshot real estate agent with famous clients. She looked up to my mother a great deal. She used to say things like, "Oh my God, you guys have, like, six homes. I love your Coldwater Canyon house. Your mom is like a big star, wheelin' and dealin'—this is awesome. I want to *be* your mother." Heidi studied for her test to get a real estate license and passed her first time, which is really difficult to do. Well, nobody ever accused Heidi of not being bright. She went to work at a real estate office right next door to Spago for a brief time.

Heidi was having an on-again, off-again relationship with the owner of Max Modeling Agency, and she started to work at his office to keep a closer eye on him. Her older man was surrounded by beautiful women and cheated on her constantly. Bernie Cornfeld was his name, and he and Heidi had a very up and down relationship. But they loved each other and Bernie was very generous: he gave her a convertible Mustang and flew her all over the world.

I was involved in my own tumultuous relationship with a great-looking model named Todd, and Heidi and I used to commiserate with each other all the time about our boyfriends. Todd had a bit of an alcohol and drug problem, which didn't seem like as much of a problem as it should have to me back then, as we all loved to party. He also had a bit of a violence problem, leading to some really scary fights.

Around this time I was looking for a roommate, and Heidi was looking to get away from Bernie. When she offered to move in with me I was thrilled. We were best friends already, why not live together?

The Party is On

Heidi was not a madam, as far as I knew, when we lived together. Once or twice she did mention something about some guy taking her shopping and going to New York, but I just said, "You go, girl." It didn't sound like prostitution; I thought she was just having fun. I can be really naïve about things sometimes.

I soon learned she was fucking James Caan. Now, this was before she was a madam, but she was getting into the life, I guess. Though I really didn't have a clue at the time, from what I understand now she was working as a hooker toward the end of the time when we were roommates. I think she tried to keep that part of her life hidden from me because I was like a sister to her, so I didn't find out about her hooking until after she moved out.

Anyway, she was seeing James Caan, though he certainly had a very serious long-term, live-in girlfriend. One day I heard Heidi come in the door. She called out, "Hey Jen, I'm home," and a second later slammed the door to her room.

I was getting ready to go out to one of my raging parties and wanted to borrow something to wear from her, so I walked out of my room naked, just with little panties on and no top. I figured when I opened the door to her room I would cover myself with an arm over my breasts. So there I was, walking out of my room almost completely naked, and I see James Caan sitting on my couch.

I ran into her room and yelled, "Oh my God, James Caan is in our living room. Why didn't you tell me that we had *James*

Caan in our living room?" I was smiling and excited, though embarrassed.

And she said, "Oh my God, I know, isn't he so hot?"

"I'm naked," I shouted.

Heidi just laughed and said, "So what. Don't worry about it; he's high out of his mind."

I guess she was right. He was just calmly sitting and staring at my dad's poster hanging on our living room wall, which was really weird to me because James starred in *The Killer Elite* with my dad and Robert Duvall. In one sense I was honored to have him in my living room, but still, I had walked past the man almost naked.

Another time Heidi went out with him and lost some cocaine. She made me drive around and try to find this big bag of cocaine in the middle of Westwood. She'd hidden it behind a bush, only she couldn't remember *which* bush. There had been some huge three-way argument between Heidi and James and his girlfriend. Crazy, huh?

I think later this girlfriend became his wife—I know they were together a very, very long time. I was never sure exactly what went down during that fight, but I pieced together that his girl-friend was out of town and then showed up suddenly. Heidi didn't want to be caught with James Caan and the coke, so she ditched her stash in a hurry. Heidi made me go back the next day and we literally looked for this cocaine for three or four hours. I'll never forget it. The two of us drove all around Westwood, jumping in and out of the car and looking behind shrubbery. Finally I said, "Come on Heidi, this is crazy. We're never going to find it—it's like looking for a needle in a haystack!" Eventually, we gave up.

Steven Tyler

When I look back now, it was clear that prostitution was all around me when I was living with Heidi. She may not have been a madam yet, but this guy who lived next door to us, Vince Conti, was definitely a pimp.

He introduced us to two working girls who lived in the building. Now, in my opinion what you do for a living is your own business. I don't want to judge. As long as you're a good friend to me, that's all that matters. So what these two girls did for money didn't bother me, and we all became friendly. One of the girls was named April.

April told us, "I've been sleeping with Steven Tyler for awhile. I love him; he's so great in bed." Heidi and I thought that was pretty cool. Then one afternoon she called us up and said, "Do you want to see Steven Tyler? He's coming over and I'm going to fuck him right now. He's going to be arriving here in three minutes, so run look outside your window."

So me, Heidi, and a friend of ours named Debbie crammed into our small kitchen, all waiting by the window, because the kitchen was the only place we could get a decent view. A black town car pulled up and little teeny Steven Tyler slipped out and then snuck into the building. At that point all three of us rushed to our front door. We peeked out and watched him go into April's apartment.

Steven stayed in the apartment down the hall for a while and as soon as he left April's place she called and said, "He's walking out the front door right now." So we raced back into the kitchen to watch him exit the building. We watched as the town car disappeared around the corner, and then April came right over to give us the details. She was all flushed, her cheeks were glowing, and she raved, "We just fucked for like an hour-and-a-half straight. He's that big…Oh my God he's so great…"

I remember her saying that day she didn't want to take money from him because she liked him so much, but he used to put money on the table for her and say something like, "Just go shopping and buy yourself something nice." He was definitely one person she didn't want to charge.

Though April worked for Vince, I think that this was more of an extracurricular activity. I'm pretty sure Steven Tyler knew what she did for a living, but they had met back stage somewhere and taken a liking to each other. Most of the time April fucked him for free because she was so in love with him. The first time she had sex with him she said he had a magical dick. April was quite a rock star groupie. She was just madly in love with him and was thinking, "Maybe he'll leave his wife and be with me." But that's dreamland.

Friends Stopping By

One day the doorbell at our apartment rang and when I opened the door there stood my old high school friend Victoria Sellers. Surprised, I asked, "What are you doing here?" thinking she must have tracked me down.

She replied, "I'm here to see Heidi." I was taken aback, but just said, "Hmm, oh, OK." Apparently they had met at a club one night, and they quickly became inseparable. Inseparable to the point of sleeping together. But Heidi and I were still best friends. We could tell each other anything, and I do mean anything.

Like the night Heidi came in laughing, telling me about how Victoria had an ingrown hair in her genital area, and Heidi had pulled it out with the aid of a magnifying glass and tweezers. There was nothing that we wouldn't say to each other.

Another night a girlfriend and I went out to a party and we picked up Matt LeBlanc, who was wasted out of his mind. Now I was partying pretty hard myself back in those days, but I can't ever recall a time when I was slurring my words like Matt was that night. He came back to my place, where I had a video game like the kind they had in the arcades. It was Breakout, like a tennis thing, very popular back then.

Matt was trying to play the game, but he was really messed up. And let me tell you, his breath was BAD. He came over to me and said, "Come here and let me give you a kiss." I tried not to cringe, but my reaction was like, "Oh my God."

Then my girlfriend came over to me and said, "I'm going to make out with him. Is it okay if we go into your room for a little bit?"

I took her aside and said, "Let me just say something honey, before you go in the room I'm going to get you a toothbrush and toothpaste, because his breath is just scary."

So I grabbed my toothbrush and some toothpaste and handed them to Matt and said, "Hey, you might need this." He just looked at me with that Joey look on his face, like, "What's that for?" He really didn't get it, but my friend made him put some toothpaste on his finger and clean his mouth out some. I thought that was pretty funny.

Matt only did commercials and stuff back then. He hadn't gotten his big break on *Friends* yet. But to be that wasted and out of it was just sad. I guess we all have our moments—I wasn't really one to talk. I had quite a cocaine habit myself by then.

And I couldn't seem to shake Todd. Keep in mind that Todd was gorgeous, had been on the cover of *Exercise* magazine, did a lot of commercials, all that sort of thing. He used to buy me tons of jewelry and so on. Yes, we had serious problems...but I still loved him.

Heidi had found another older man shortly after leaving Bernie for good. Ivan was his name, and he was just as bad as Bernie, if not worse. I know he's the one who introduced her to Elizabeth Adams, aka Madam Alex, and I guess that was about the time she started making big plans. The three of them all spent a great deal of time together. I knew Madam Alex ran a prostitution business in LA.

Madam Alex was quite a character. She was hard-core and ballsy. Heidi used to be able to drive her into an absolute rage and profanity would just fly out of her mouth... "You cocksucker, motherfucker..." on and on. She couldn't stop herself. We used to just giggle. Heidi would poke me and say, "Watch, look at what I can make her do!" It seemed funny at the time, but looking back, the situation was actually very serious. I had no idea what Heidi was up to, but I didn't like it. The light was starting to dawn on me just exactly what kinds of activities Heidi was into. I told myself that she was hanging out with her boyfriend and maybe he was up to some kind of seedy stuff. She did her best to keep things from me, but I could see that she was entering a whole new world.

My Idols

One of the best parties Heidi and I ever went to was thrown by Stevie Nicks. My mom leased her a $20 million dollar estate in Beverly Hills and knew how much I idolized the singer, so she brought me along to take the final house tour before Stevie moved in. I was so starstruck that I couldn't even speak. Toward the end of the tour I was finally able to mumble a few words. Being tongue-tied had happened before with men, but that was the first time I had literally been unable to speak to another woman.

Heidi called me all excited one day, saying we were going to some amazing party that night, and that Billy Idol was going to be there. She knew I was crazy for Billy Idol. Heidi, Debbie and I drove up the winding hills and Heidi kept teasing me about a surprise as we pulled up to the valet parkers. We got out of the car and I realized, "Hey, this is Stevie Nicks' place—my mom leased it to her!"

As soon as I exited the car and was standing on the driveway, Heidi covered my eyes with her hands—and when I turned around Billy Idol was standing right in front of me. Heidi whispered something to him, and he came up to me and sang directly into my ear. His lips were actually touching my ear as he slowly sang "Rebel Yell" to me. My face turned bright red...I was dying. I couldn't believe it. Billy Idol was #1 on every chart, the hottest thing there was. Heidi really could be a good friend sometimes.

The party had a theme: Alice in Wonderland. Stevie Nicks was dressed as Alice and all the staff was dressed as various other characters from the book. It was the most elaborate party I had ever seen—right down to the checkerboard floor.

I was on a sober kick at that time and had almost 90 days' sobriety. As the party wound down, Heidi and Billy invited me to come into the recording studio with them to work on his latest record. I knew that drugs would be all over the place, so I turned it down. It was the hardest thing I ever did. I knew I wasn't strong enough to resist the mounds of blow that would be all over the place. They all tried to talk me into going for at least an hour, and I refused, even though I wanted to go so badly. I wound up having a slip a week later, which was really annoying.

Tokyo

Our friend Debbie was a model and Pauly Shore's girlfriend at the time. Heidi had met her on a plane coming back from New York. It was very funny, really. Heidi had a copy of *Penthouse* magazine with her picture on the cover, and there Debbie was, live and in person, sitting across the aisle from her. Debbie is blonde, but had worn a black wig for that cover shoot. Heidi kept looking at the magazine cover, to the girl, back to the magazine, and finally said, "Hey, this is you!"

Debbie was from Illinois, but the next thing you know, Heidi brought this girl home. They hung out all the time—like the day we all spied on Steven Tyler—and I'm sure, looking back, that they, too were fooling around together.

Even though I was partying hard, I had always been focused on singing and was working hard on my career. I put together an act with Debbie and we booked a gig in Tokyo. I had a good voice; Debbie's OK, but two blondes singing in Tokyo were a big attraction. The owner of the nightclub liked Debbie and saw me as carrying most of the singing.

Just before I left for Tokyo, I was headed out on a modeling go-see. I forgot a picture, and I came back to the apartment and found Heidi on the phone with my boyfriend Todd lying on the floor at her feet, buck naked. I couldn't believe my eyes. I hadn't been gone two minutes. They both swore they were just playing around. Heidi really could talk me into believing anything. Obviously.

Todd and I had been together, off and on, for four rocky years by now. I tried to break up with Todd for good before I left for Tokyo. We got into a violent argument. He wasn't taking "no" for an answer, and he grabbed me and held me upside down. If he had dropped me, my neck would have snapped. Heidi raced in and convinced him to set me down and calmed him a bit. To this day I believe Heidi saved me; she really did. The situation with Todd remained unresolved, though I did tell him before I left that we were through.

I had a three-day fling with Grant Show in New York just before I left for Tokyo, but that was because I had been hearing all sorts of things about Todd. I knew that Victoria Sellers had given Todd a blow job in my first apartment! So did the lead singer from Missing Persons! I had heard things about Todd before more than once. I got a little bit of revenge with Grant. In my mind, I had ended it before I left, but in Todd's eyes were were still together.

Debbie and I got into an argument while we were in Tokyo— Debbie was getting a little jealous about the whole singing thing, and she blurted out angrily, "You think Heidi's your best friend? I don't think she's your best friend." I was like, "Debbie, what are you talking about?"

"She's fucking Todd, you know." It was a shot to the heart. I wasn't into Heidi in any sexual way, but I loved her as a friend dearly. I loved her just about as much as I loved my boyfriend Todd. The three of us had done things together all the time, for years. I thought they had a great brother/sister-type relation-ship. I was beyond livid.

I called Heidi from Tokyo and started screaming. "I want you to move out. Be gone when I get back. How could you do this to me?" I was crying, and I had never heard Heidi cry as hard as she did that day. "Oh my God Jen, it's not true, I'm going to kill Debbie; I'm going to fucking kill her!" she screamed. "I'm going to ruin her!" Heidi said, *"Because she's done some work for me, you know."*

And oh my God, did she get Debbie, but good. Pauly Shore was calling Debbie every day in Tokyo. I didn't know it, but Debbie had just started working for Heidi and done a few jobs, like going on Adnan Khashoggi's yacht. She'd done maybe three or four jobs and Heidi knew that Pauly was completely in the dark about that part of her life. But that was about to end, because Heidi told me on the phone that she was "going to tell Pauly EVERYTHING."

My mind started racing. I was panicked. I thought, "Oh my God, oh my God, this is going to screw up everything in Tokyo! We're already having so many problems."

I was angry at everyone—Todd, Heidi, Debbie. I was so pissed at Debbie I yelled, "I think *you* fucked my boyfriend too! I think you all three fucked each other! Fuck all of you!" I was just furious. When I had heard rumors about Victoria and Todd I was pissed, but Heidi was a whole different story. She was my best friend, I was living with her, and she knew I was having serious problems with my boyfriend. After I heard this about Heidi, there was no way I was willing to try to work things out with him.

And the craziest thing was that Todd really was obsessed with me; when I tried to break up with him he tried to commit suicide. I couldn't understand it, because he was fucking everything that moved, though he swore he was in love with me.

Heidi did tell Pauly all about Debbie—that his girlfriend was a call girl. Boy, did everything change. Debbie was really in love with Pauly... she adored him, just like I loved Todd. Pauly was very freaked out, he and Debbie had been very much in love.

All this drama was going down and meanwhile, Debbie and I still had to work together and finish out the gig in Tokyo. Finally, we got back to LA. Heidi talked to Pauly and we all got together and forgave each other. I forgave Heidi, but I absolutely did not want to be with Todd anymore. It was over.

Heidi Moves Out

The other big problem I had with living with Heidi was that I really wanted to get sober. I was doing a lot of cocaine, and Heidi wasn't ready to get clean. I had told her, before I left for Tokyo, that she needed to get clean or I couldn't live with her anymore. We had some serious talks about getting our acts together. She swore there would be no more drugs in the house, which wasn't exactly the case.

I found this out because Pauly and Debbie told me; they both knew I was trying to get straight, and were probably still a little pissed about the whole Tokyo incident. They told me that Heidi was still using. Debbie said, "Look if you don't believe me, I know exactly where her stash is. Trust me; she's got ounces right here in your house."

I couldn't believe it, but they dropped by and Debbie casually asked Heidi, "So, you're not partying anymore, right?" Heidi said, "No, I told Jen I wasn't going to anymore, and that's that." Debbie went straight to the closet and pulled out a huge mound of blow and plopped it down.

I was so angry. Heidi was like, "That's not mine, it's for some of my friends…" On and on. But she was so busted. Pauly and Debbie flushed the coke down the toilet right in front of us. Heidi freaked out, trying to stop Pauly and save her drugs, but it was too late.

Heidi's boyfriend Ivan was another real problem. He used to call and threaten us. He would call my number at five in the morning and say threatening things. One night it was, "Why don't you tell Heidi to go check her car!"

After that particular call we went downstairs to the garage and saw that he had destroyed her orange BMW. Taken a hammer to it, knocked out the windshield, slashed the tires, you name it.

The drugs, Ivan, the whole incident with Todd...we had to separate. She told me she was going to move out; that her father was helping her buy a house. "Don't be upset Jen, it's all for the best. We'll still be close." I was sad to see her go, but I also knew it was healthier and the best thing for me. Heidi moved to a small house in West Hollywood on West Knoll, I found another roommate and life continued on.

The Madam

Heidi had a lot of problems in those days, not just drugs and a bad boyfriend. She and I used to go to the horse races a lot, just for fun, I thought. I used to jump for joy if I won a hundred bucks. I didn't realize the severity of Heidi's gambling habit. It was out of control. After she moved out I stopped by her new place and found it completely empty. I asked, "Where's all the furniture?"

She said, "Oh, I had to pay it as a gambling debt."

After Heidi moved out of the apartment we shared, we remained very close friends. As I said, I don't judge my friends, it was fine with me; she could do what she wanted to do—which, it was becoming clear, was be a madam. When I needed a job, Heidi suggested I go to work for Madam Alex. She needed someone to buy cat food for her, for one thing; there must have been 50 cats in that place.

Madam Alex was a recluse; she never left her house. All she did was sit inside and sniff Kleenex with cocaine in it. I found my new job a little strange. I used to see the most gorgeous girls coming in and out. Madam Alex's son was always coming and going, and Ivan and Heidi were around a lot too, although they were always arguing. They would give me money to go run errands. A few times I took Madam Alex to the market just to get her out of the house, like Heidi wanted me to.

As time went on she started sharing more and more with me about what she was doing. "They're going to be writing books about me one day!" she told me. She always had a cocky attitude. One day we were out driving in her black Corvette convertible and she turned to me with a smile on her face and told me that she was a madam. I was surprised to hear her say it flat out so boldly, but hey, it was her life. She had the right to live it any way she wanted. I still loved her as a friend.

After that she started to tell me everything. I'd had inklings of this stuff before, like when she told Pauly that Debbie worked for her, but now all the cards were on the table and she shared every business detail with me. I heard more about all about how she sent girls to see Arab princes on yachts and that they were getting 20 to 30 grand a pop for a weekend.

One day she said, "I've got to get some girls together to see Oliver North." This was right around the time of the Iran Contra scandal.

"Come on, Jen," she mused, "I need two girls to send to Virginia to see Oliver North. I'm going to send two, just in case he doesn't like one. Or maybe he'll want to see both of them."

Oliver, she said, was one of her biggest clients. She had everyone calling her, huge heavyweights in the entertainment industry. It was an open secret that Michael Eisner was one of her clients. I heard the Eisner name a lot, and I was introduced to him several times, though I didn't even know it was him. Then there was Billy Idol—I remember him refusing to pay, because he was a rock star-but I really was oblivious to most of it. I would see these people at her parties, but to me, if they weren't young and hot, I didn't care. I didn't think too much about these super big-time people who were hanging out at her place.

"Can you believe the secrets I know?" she asked me one day. "I could own the world! I could destroy the world! I have FBI agents on my side!" and she showed me the business card of an FBI agent. She told me some of them were her friends.

The funny thing is that her work actually kind of put a burden on our friendship because she was stuck at home, running her business. She could get girls to stay home with her and do whatever she wanted, but I wanted to still go out and party and have a good time. Before she was a madam we would go out and hang out and do all these fun things. Sure, there were nights when she could still get out, but it was starting to become rarer.

By this time Heidi was at the height of her career I had gone through a couple of relationships, but she was still stuck like glue to Ivan.

I had moved on from Todd and was with a new boyfriend. I went out with this horrible guy John for awhile—he was actually the only guy who has ever hurt me, he popped me in the face when he was drunk. He gave me a bloody eye, and Heidi took me to the hospital the next day. I ran through John pretty quickly though and wound up with Kevin. We both loved to party and had incredible sex—it seemed like a great match.

Running Madam's Errands

Eventually, after Heidi took over Madam Alex's business, she said to me, "Come work for me, running errands. Number one, you're the only one I trust. These girls...some of them don't have IDs, many of them I don't trust, so what you can do is run my errands, go get my lunch, that kind of stuff."

So I went to work for her as an assistant. Heidi used to pay me in cash, either $50 or $100 a day, sometimes three days a week, sometimes four. This was when she lived on West Knoll in West Hollywood, in the early 1990s. It was just errand running, picking stuff up like her favorite perfume, Chanel No. 5. I remember once they accidentally gave me Chanel No. 19 and she threw a fit; I had to go back to the store and get her the right bottle. I also used to go to the bank alot; I was in charge of cashing all the girls' checks.

A lot of her clients used to write checks to CASH or made out directly to Heidi Fleiss, and I was the one who took them to the bank to cash them. Many of them, I noticed, were signed by Charlie Sheen.

I didn't like doing this, and I said, "Listen Heidi, I'm scared."

She told me not to worry. "I've got it all under control...I'm paying you a hundred bucks, just run the errand. All you have to do is show your ID at the bank, get the money, bring it back, and that's it!"

I kept saying, "Are you sure I won't get in any trouble?"

"Jen, he's my friend," Heidi told me. "This could be for anything!" These were big checks, four and five and seven thousand dollars a pop.

Sometimes I would leave the bank with $20,000 cash in my purse. I used to race back to her place and hand it over. Heidi really trusted me, obviously. I wouldn't have dreamed of taking any of the money; I just wanted to get rid of it.

I used to go to the bank all the time and sign the backs of Charlie Sheen's checks. The bank people used to give me funny looks. There were others, of course, like Texas billionaire businessman Robert T. Crow. But Charlie stuck out in my mind, because he was so famous. I can't even count the number of checks I cashed for him, but I never once met the guy. Maybe I saw him at a party once, but I felt like I knew him. Honestly, you would have thought we were married, with all the checks I cashed for Charlie. He was one of her best clients the whole time she was in business.

Because I was hanging around with Heidi all the time and running her errands, I used to hear a lot of the inner workings of her business. The most hysterical thing was all the girls coming in all the time saying, "Heidi, I love working for you, it's been great, but I had such a great time with Charlie and he asked me to marry him. So I don't think I'll be working for you any more. I just need to let you know."

Heidi would just laugh, because she heard it all the time! From all her girls! She said, "Jen, if I had a hundred bucks for every girl who said this to me, I'd be rich." One time, hearing this speech for what must have been the hundredth time, she got so frustrated she screamed, "I can't take this anymore! You're a hooker, he doesn't like you, and you're not getting married! This is the 20th proposal he's made THIS YEAR! Sorry!!!"

This one poor girl was just in tears; she couldn't believe it. But it had gotten on Heidi's nerves, having to let all these girls down gently.

I continued to run Heidi's errands. One day she mentioned there was a really wealthy Mexican oil tycoon from a super-rich family in town, and she said, "Jen, you could get like 40 grand and a Rolex! But he likes to take showers, so you would have to pee on him." I said, "Heidi, there is no way. You couldn't pay me enough."

I could not do something like that. It was a ton of money back then though. This was the first and only time she brushed something like that by me. I said, "Heidi, you know me, you know I could never do something like that!"

"OK, OK, just thought I'd run it by you. No big deal." She didn't push. She didn't need to; there was no shortage of women wanting to work for her. Including Victoria Sellers, though they kept it very hush-hush at the time.

Heidi always became very close to her top girls. They would either be living with her or spending all their time with her. She used to have two or three top girls at a time, and they'd get the most work and the best clients, but as soon as they screwed her over, she'd find new girls. And more than a few of them did stab her in the back.

Eventually she moved into a house in Benedict Canyon. One of her girls had gotten robbed at gunpoint in front of her West Hollywood house, so she needed better security. She thought it was just a story, that one of the girls was trying to get around giving her the 40% commission, but then Heidi actually got robbed herself in her own yard. She realized she had to get out of there. She was making a lot of money and cash was all over the place; it was not safe.

And there I was, still cashing the checks. I kept worrying, saying, "Heidi, are you sure this is all right?" She kept saying it was fine, these people who wrote the checks were her friends, she was running an escort service, nothing illegal…over and over. She kept trying to calm me down. I hated going to that bank, but I needed the hundred bucks she was paying me to run her errands. Plus, of course, we were still great friends.

After she got her new house up in the hills I used to swim with her all the time at the pool in Benedict Canyon. Looking back, I can't believe I did this, but despite the whole Todd incident, Heidi was still like a sister to me. I trusted her. I would bring Kevin up to her house and Heidi and I would both swim topless in front of him. At the time I really was OK with it, but looking back, I'm not sure what I was thinking.

Heidi had a lot of girls in those days and they were all breathtaking. I remember one of her top girls, Samantha, being especially gorgeous. She had everyone in love with her, including Heidi and Axl Rose, both at the same time. Samantha had been a Chanel runway model, but really, one of Heidi's girls was more gorgeous than the next. You would look at one and think, "There's *no way* this girl could be a hooker."

Heidi was very picky about perfection. Even without makeup, all her girls were flawless. Heidi herself was not a flawless beauty, but she had something about her, a magnetism, a very grabbing personality. She was smart, persuasive, funny, attractive, very quick-witted, and always fun to be around.

Heidi loved the money, but she would hook up with these girls and get very attached to them. In a strange kind of irony, she would send them out on jobs, but at the same time get a little jealous of what they were doing and who they were doing it with. She really took a fancy to quite a few of them.

And the girls wanted more than anything to be part of her innermost clique. I remember a couple of new girls hanging out at her house on Benedict—Michael Douglas's old house—and they were desperate to be one of her top girls. They would bend over backwards, do anything, wear the skimpiest clothes, anything to get Heidi's attention. Those girls wanted to be the new Samantha. The competition was fierce because the top girls got the best clients, and that meant a lot of money.

One girl came right out and asked me, "What do I have to do? What the hell do I have to do? Why is Heidi always trying to find Samantha, when I'm standing right here? What's it going to take to get in her good graces?"

Sure, there was a lot of money, but there was always loads of drama to match it. Plenty of these girls were screwing her over financially. It happened all the time. Heidi used to tell me stories about how they often would be paid a lot of money in cash, and they'd keep most of it and not give Heidi her 40%. I think that was a big reason she wanted to start taking checks. Cash made it tricky, and she used to have huge fights with these girls.

She was stuck, because she needed the girls, but they were screwing her over. She would catch them all the time and call them on it, because the guys would call Heidi and say, "She was great, I gave her ten thousand dollars!" Heidi would be livid, because the girl had told her she got seven. There was lots of intrigue and deceit and mind games all over the place back them.

Frankly, I think Heidi got in over her head. I could not believe this was the girl I used to go swimming with and spend nights with at her condo. The girl I would bake cookies with and ride bicycles with! Sometimes she would yell at me, and I would say, "Heidi, don't yell at ME. This is ME you're talking to, Jen, remember?"

Unfortunately, around that time she also picked up a pretty heavy crystal meth habit, which can really screw people up. It had a lot to do with really messing her up. Crystal meth was a habit Ivan introduced her to. Honestly, I never understood their relationship. She used to say about Ivan, "He's just gross, you can see the dirt under his fingernails." She was always putting him down, but when he called, she ran, and then she'd come back black and blue. She was sexually hooked on him; she could not tear herself away. All I wanted was for her to leave Ivan, I was really worried about her when she was with him.

Sometimes, once in awhile, the old Heidi would come back for a little while, and she would say things to me like, "Jen, I don't want you around this kind of stuff. I'm sorry..."

Party Girl

I really was a party girl in those days. In fact, I was featured in *Cosmopolitan* magazine as the number one party girl in town. Hard Copy featured me on a 30-second spot and they said the ratings were so high that they aired it two nights later and they made it into an almost seven-minute segment.

I had a lot of fun in those days. Sometimes I would end up at parties and not know anybody there. It was exciting; you wouldn't know where you're going to end up or what you'd be doing. As long as it was fun and there were drugs and alcohol and cute guys, I was good. I wouldn't even care how I'd get home.

I loved to go out and be invited to great parties and hang out and see what was going on. It was a lot of drugs and drinking and craziness; I'll never forget one particular New Year's Eve party. Heidi was screaming my name. She lost me somehow; she went one way and I went the other. So she just started screaming my name until we found each other, and we thought that was just hilarious.

At that time in my life I was more interested in going front row and backstage to concerts and hanging out and getting high than I was in my own career. Sometimes it makes me upset now because I really think I could have done a hell of a lot more with my life if I had not been so involved in the party scene. My mother knew some high-ups at the corporate Victoria's Secret office, and I blew off not one but two modeling interviews with them. I couldn't have cared less at the time, but I look back and have to wonder what was I thinking.

But you know what—it was fun. I had a great fucking time. Plus, I had the most incredible sex I've ever had in my life while on cocaine.

I was still with my boyfriend Kevin—we stayed together for five years. Our relationship was totally cocaine induced. And it was really scary because there were a couple times that things got pretty bad. He would be on the floor throwing up or passed out and then, luckily, he'd be okay. We'd be right back doing drugs two nights later.

Once he gave me head for five hours and I literally had to pull him off of me saying, "I'm going to have nothing left down there."

When you are high you think that it's great sex, but really, it was just excessive. I was definitely addicted to sex and cocaine at that time in my life. One went hand in hand with the other.

Rick James used to throw huge parties. Tons of people would be there, hanging out, drinking, doing drugs, having a great time, but without their host. It would take three hours before he would actually come out. Rick would have pictures of himself everywhere, his music would be playing, and there would be huge buffet tables for everyone. Finally, only after the scene was set, he would come out.

I was at one of these parties up in the Hollywood Hills when he was dating Debbie, who was Heidi's ex-girlfriend, by then Pauly Shore's ex-girlfriend, and now Rick James's ex-girlfriend. Can anyone say "six-degrees of separation?"

I was having a great time at one of his parties when he finally came out and graced everyone with his presence one evening. He was all dressed up in stage clothing. He put "Super Freak" on the sound system and started singing for everyone. He called out to me, "Come on, Jen, come up here and sing." So Rick James and I belted out "Super Freak" together, which I thought was really cool and really fun, especially because it was right around the time M.C. Hammer remade his hit with "Can't Touch This." This was the kind of night I loved back then.

Rick James was such a party animal. Sometimes his parties would go all night and not break up until four o'clock the next afternoon. And sometimes I'd bring friends up there to see him and he'd tell whoever was at his house, "Okay, Jennifer's coming up, if I'm sleeping just give this and this to her." It would be like a little mound of blow and a bag of weed.

I in turn would tell whoever was there to give him what I brought him. I used to cook barbequed chicken, salad, mashed potatoes, and corn. I'd make him up a big plate and carry it up to the house. I would sit there and party with my friends and just hang out. Then, a couple of days later he would call and say he had inhaled my food. He used to say, "You Jewish girls are such good cooks. You really know what the hell you're doing. Let me tell you, that's damn good chicken, girl."

I was hanging around with him a lot pretty close to the time he was arrested and sent to jail for raping a girl. It was very hard core, a lot of awful stuff came out in the press, like he'd raped her with a knife. I had been right there at his house, partying away, oblivious to what was going on just two nights after he had done this. Eventually he was convicted for aggravated assault and false imprisonment for things he did to two women; some of the charges dated all the way back to 1991.

I remember running into him after he got out of jail in 1995. I gave him the biggest hug, because that could have been me he hurt. That so easily could have been me, but he respected me enough not to do that to me.

The Music Biz

Of course, I did more with my life than hang out with Heidi, run her errands, and party. I have always been a singer and I love performing, though I think the business side of the industry stinks. I just remember being really frustrated with the music business back then. Basically, the only way you were going to get a record deal was if you gave it up. For instance: Back in the mid-nineties Maurice Starr was putting together an all-girl band.

Maurice was a huge music mogul. He'd produced a bunch of acts, including New Kids on the Block and New Edition. Anyway, he was set up at the penthouse at the Four Seasons (where the president stayed when he was in town) and used to have all these girls over and serve everyone plenty of champagne. I remember seeing one girl, who couldn't have been a day over 18, coming out of his room. Basically, she was saying, "If you ain't giving it up, you ain't getting no deal."

I visited his penthouse a couple of times. Once he put his arms around me and put his hands near my breasts. The mood was definitely set with the champagne flowing and a seemingly endless supply of caviar. The story was, basically, that he'd sign you, but he wanted to fool around with you too. And I wasn't about to do it. The same thing had happened with another producer, Jimmy George. All these producers wanted to get into my pants.

And things haven't changed much. About seven years ago Tiffany's manager, George Tobin, did the same kind of thing, except he didn't actually want to get into my pants as much as he wanted to tear me down. He belittled me badly. "You need this to be changed. Your face needs to be changed, you need a nose job, you need to lose weight, you need to have this done, you need to have that done. "

He would say things to me like, "Where were you 10 years ago when Tiffany was around? You would have been perfect and now you're older. But damn, you've got a voice—what power and tone."

I actually believed he wanted to work with me, because I spent an exhausting ten-hour day meeting with him. The problem came when, after I had been there for more than 8 hours already, he gave me a song to learn. Unfortunately the song was in French and he told me I only had 45 minutes to learn it and sing it back to him—in French, of course, which I don't speak. I left there in tears, just crying my eyes out. I had been so hopeful. The music business is tough, and it certainly hasn't gotten any easier through all the years I've been in it—but nothing was going to stop me from my dream.

by Olivia, Carly, Amanda, and Jennifer

The Downfall of Madam Fleiss

The night everything changed between Heidi and me started out on a nice note. I had been really upset with her because she failed to invite me to a great party she threw for Mick Jagger. We had squabbled about that and my feelings were still hurt, so she called me up and said, "Look, I really am sorry. I'm having a big party at the Rangoon Racquet Club tonight."

It was Samantha's birthday, and she was trying hard to smooth things over between us. "I want you to come, please come out." I asked her if I could bring a couple girlfriends and she said, "Sure."

I remember circling around the block endlessly that night, trying to find a parking spot. A red Ferrari was behind me, also looking for a parking space, and it followed me around for awhile. didn't think anything of it. Finally I went to the valet. Once I got inside the party, this guy from the Ferrari came right up to me. I was high; at the time I was still partying, running to the bathroom to do a couple of bumps of coke.

This guy told me his name was Sammy Lee and asked if he could buy me a drink. I told him I wasn't interested, that I had a boyfriend, and went back into the bathroom. When I came back out he was sitting at a table with the girlfriends I had brought with me. I thought, "What does he want? Why won't he buzz off?"

He said right off the bat as soon as I approached the table, "Listen, I'm here from Hawaii, and I'm looking to buy a house in the $4 million range in the flats of Beverly Hills." Now *that* got my attention, because my mom was in real estate and paid me referral fees. So I warmed up and started telling this guy all about my mom. I literally called her from the party and said I had found her a client. Then Sammy said, "I'd really like to meet the girl who's throwing this party. I've never seen so many beautiful girls in one place!"

I said, "Sure, she's one of my best friends." So I walked over and grabbed Heidi and introduced them. That was it. I told Heidi he was looking for a house. I explained that I was going to turn him onto my mom, and he had wanted to meet the girl who was throwing this party. It was just in passing, a quick introduction. I went back to the party and didn't think anything more about it.

Two days later, I got a phone call from Heidi. "Jen," she said, "that guy that you introduced me to is an undercover cop, and I have been in jail for the past couple days."

Her words threw me into a complete state of shock. I couldn't imagine what had happened; she was on and off, on and off with Ivan all the time. He could be such a bastard that I thought he might be behind this. Heidi was beyond upset. Not only was she arrested that night, but someone had flooded her entire house while she was gone. All her beautiful hardwood floors were ruined.

Heidi was angry with me, but I said, "Look, that guy I intro-duced you to was driving a Ferrari! I saw him before we got into the party! He told me he was looking for a house! How would an undercover cop be driving a Ferrari?"

I hung up the phone and could not believe what I had just heard. How horrible was that? The undercover cop baited me perfectly—he set the trap just right with that whole real estate thing. To this day I don't know who set that up.

I was an innocent pawn in all of this, but Heidi was high and surrounded by people who were high, and they were all telling her it had to have been me who set her up. After all the shit we had been through, the ups and downs, I told her she was out of her freaking mind to even think for a second I would have done something like that to her. Sometimes when we talked she would believe me, other times she'd think I really had set her up and would have Ivan call and threaten me. It was all so crazy and dramatic.

When the scandal broke everyone was after me. I was on the cover of the Los Angeles Times; news vans followed me every-where for weeks. Thank God the first Michael Jackson scandal came along, because it finally gave everyone something else to focus on. It was awful. I used to cry to my mother, "I didn't do anything wrong! All I did was run errands for her!"

Heidi Wear

After all that went down Heidi and I didn't talk for a long time. Then, almost a year after it all went down, I ended up being the cover story in *BUZZ* magazine, which was pretty big at the time. They labeled me a party girl, which I must admit I still certain-ly was back then. More importantly to me, they also said I had an amazing voice and that I could be a big singing star.

The interviewer had asked me some questions about Heidi, and I said a couple of very nice things about her. She read the arti-cle, and called me up. By time she had a clothing store in

Pasadena and asked me if I needed a job; she said I could come and work with her.

Nothing was really ever quite the same between us, though. I tried hard to make everything right again, but there was this doubt in the back of her mind that I could not get rid of. She closed the Pasadena store and opened up one in the Promenade in Santa Monica. She knew I was smart, and wanted my opinion on the right retail space. I helped her find the new space, and went to work at the new store too. I was bending over backwards, kissing her ass—I was always her best salesgirl. Once I sold $4,000 worth of clothes! In one day! It was a very happening store—Heidiwear was very popular among celebrities.

At that point, Heidi was dating an older woman who lived in the old Elvis Presley estate in Trousdale. I could not believe my eyes when I saw her new lover. This woman was quite a few years older. But Heidi used to show up wearing the most beautiful jewelry, fine estate pieces that this woman would give her. Heidi told me some gross sexual story about how this woman had farted in her face when they were fooling around. Even if things had changed, there was still nothing we couldn't tell each other.

I really held down the fort at the store, because Heidi was busy meeting with her lawyers all the time. Whenever she returned from one of those sessions I knew seeing my face reminded her of the whole situation and how she had been brought down. I was a loyal friend, I was doing whatever I could to show it, but the bottom line was we could not get past what happened. It made me sad; it hurt me, but I believe now that Heidi knows in her heart of hearts that I had nothing to do with that set-up.

I stayed working for Heidi right until the bitter end—when she made a deal and went to jail. Obviously, the store closed when she started her sentence. Heidi had a tremendous amount of support among her clientele and L.A. residents in general. Everyone was so mad—what had she done that was so bad she needed to serve time, while all the customers got off scot-free?

I wrote Heidi a heartfelt five-page letter while she was in jail, telling her how sorry I was about what had happened to her and reaffirming once again how I would always be her friend. I sprayed the stationery with Chanel No. 5. But she never replied, and I never heard from her again when she was released.

Cold Turkey

My boyfriend Kevin and I had been partying hard together for years by this time. One of the things that snapped me back into a drug-free life was seeing regular people on the street after we had been partying all night long, waking up at two o'clock in the afternoon and then having breakfast at four. I would go out after that and be driving aimlessly in my car, seeing regular people all around me and realizing there was nothing normal about the way I lived my life.

I was tired of chasing the high. I loved that feeling when you first do a line of cocaine. But you can't really get that first-line high again once you do cocaine regularly, and I was tired of spending all my time looking for that feeling again. It wasn't ever going to happen. Cocaine had really hurt me—I came close to overdosing more than once. By this point I was angry.

I was so angry at what cocaine had done to my life that I didn't want to do it anymore.

I had been to a few meetings and I understood what the AA program was all about, but this time I decided to do it myself. And I did it, I quit doing cocaine cold turkey. I'm making it sound easy, when it really wasn't—but the decision was simple. Live or die. That's the decision I had to make. I put the drugs down and never did another line to this day.

After I quit I realized that I would have to give up other parts of my life to stay healthy. Kevin and I split, and I started seeing a guy much younger than me after I'd become sober. He was great in bed, but he was on cocaine. So I had to wait for him to do his last line so I could get him into bed. I started thinking, "God, this is too much for me. Everyone's doing cocaine but me and here I am trying to find the hot, cute guys."

So, I stopped looking for guys that did drugs. I just knew that, too, could no longer be a part of my life. The party girl quit partying. I am very grateful to be sober now. I've been away from cocaine for almost 11 years now. Seriously, I don't know how I did it. I was not as bad of a user as everybody else was around me, but it was clearly bad enough for me. For people who are out there and struggling with drug problems, there is hope. You've just got to make the choice, live or die.

Injury

Even though I was an active addict for a long time, what really waylaid me wasn't drugs, but a nerve disorder. It started as a simple accident—I sliced my foot into a nail—but wound up taking over my life for years.

I got a record deal just before this happened. Things were going great, I was touring and then this accident happened and it was like I literally went from the stage to a wheelchair in the blink of an eye. That shows you just how precious life is. That's how quickly your life can change. My life pretty much ground to a halt for five or six years as I battled my injury and the resulting complications. The suffering I've been through has been tough, but I actually think it made me a much stronger person. I think it changed me in so many ways for the better.

The minor injury turned into a chronic neurological disorder that got so bad I was actually in a wheelchair for a time. I was really ill; I had to walk on crutches when I could walk at all; some days I could barely get out of bed. I had beaten my cocaine addiction only to be brought down by this rare disorder. The pain was all-consuming and never stopped. For the first time in my life I considered suicide—the pain was that bad. I thought of my dad—often—and had a new understanding and sympathy for him. I truly understood that he felt he had no other choice but to check out. This was a huge revelation to me.

At my lowest point I looked at my rows of medication and really thought about checking out myself. If it wasn't for God I don't think I would have been able to get through it. I was literally counting out the pills. It crossed my mind that I'm too claustrophobic to be shut up in a small dark coffin; then I said to myself, "You'll be dead, you schmuck!"

But then I thought seriously about what it would be like not to have any more orgasms, and what it would be like to not eat pizza. I also thought about what it was like to be in a dark room because I could not take the pain anymore. And that was it. I don't know how I did it but I just somehow got myself out of the wheelchair and stepped down on my foot over and over again to desensitize it. I can't even explain that kind of pain.

That was the turning point. I decided that no matter what, I was going to make myself have some kind of life. I yearned to do something, anything—for years I had been at home writing a script, practicing singing, and suffering through the pain. The party girl had become practically a hermit. I knew that had to change. I needed to get back out there and be around people again. A casual friend brought this fact home to me one day.

She called me up and said to me, "You know, you're not dead. You might be ill and you're in a wheelchair, but you're not dead. Get up and get the fuck *out*."

So Simona came and picked me up in a limo and told me that we were going to pick the rest of the people up at an address I recognized because an ex-boyfriend, Jed Leiber, had moved there. Jed was a big music producer, and my favorite ex-boyfriend ever—my mom was crazy about him. Jed was the son of Jerry Lieber of the legendary songwriting team of Lieber and Stoller, who had written *Hound Dog*, *Stand By Me* and many other hits for Elvis. I'd had a great time with Jed; he introduced me to so many brilliant musicians: Mick Jagger and Keith Richards, Jeff Beck, Roy Orbison (who whispered, "Hello, Pretty Woman" in my ear when we were introduced). I thought of all the good times I'd had as the limo idled in front of the building; I was glad I was finally getting out again. We loaded a bunch of girls into the limo and headed to the party.

I couldn't believe it when we got there. It was like I had entered a time warp. Because I was on crutches, I thanked God that one of my girlfriends, who is six feet tall, was with me. I was really kind of scared and nervous, but she could scan the crowd for me.

Even though I was anxious, I was also glad to be out of the house and getting around on my crutches. I was just sitting there and the next thing I knew someone was running up to me and saying, "Heidi's here." And then I saw it was Victoria Sellers. She was so wasted she could barely talk, but she was trying to bring Heidi and me together to make up.

I was happy to see Victoria, but I felt badly that she was high out of her mind and so, so skinny. Heidi, too. For whatever reason, I didn't feel comfortable seeing Heidi at the time and didn't want to rekindle the friendship. It was clear that nothing had changed. Everyone was still partying and getting high. I don't know how they were living; some of the people around them looked like the walking dead. It was unbelievable; I could almost see right through some of them. Heidi and I never spoke that night.

When Heidi came out of jail she seemed to keep a low profile for a little while, but it seemed to me that she started right up again. From what I hear she is back in the same business, but she's gone legit. She's running the first-ever legal brothel in Australia and starting up a brothel for women in Las Vegas called the Stud Farm. She even has a line of Hollywood Madam clothing, and she's also currently on the New York Stock Exchange, which blows my mind.

Basically nothing has changed, except now she doesn't get into trouble for what she does. Even her on-again off-again relationship with Tom Sizemore was a lot like the relationship she had with Ivan. It may not be good for her, but I guess that's not illegal.

The last time I saw Heidi was at the skin care spa we both go to—Nance Mitchell, facialist to the stars. I was walking in when I saw her driving by. She didn't see me, and I didn't try to get her attention.

Howard Stern

One of the coolest things I ever did was to be a guest on the Howard Stern show in 2000. I had to go to his studio in a wheelchair because of my foot injury, but nothing would have stopped me. He wanted me on the show because I had been voted one of the 25 sexiest women, along with Jennifer Lopez, of 1999 in *Celebrity Sleuth* magazine. Howard saw this because his favorite magazines are *Playboy*, *Penthouse* and *Celebrity Sleuth*. I sent him a CD of me singing before my appearance.

When he introduced me he said my father was in one of the best movies of all time, "They Shoot Horses, Don't They?" I was on the air with Howard for 90 minutes and he talked a lot about what was going on in my life and what I was doing. It was pretty exciting. He was very respectful of me and my music and played a remix of me singing the KISS classic "I Was Made For Loving You." Howard loved it—so much that he told me he was going to try to get me a record deal.

The 90 minutes flew by, and as time went on I just started falling in love with him. In between commercial takes he was a completely different person than he was on the show.

I had a manicure that day and it said "Howard Rules" on my nails. I was just smitten with him. And as the show went on I thought, "Oh my God I'm in love with this guy. I know he's taken, but I'm just frickin' in love with him."

I had a boyfriend, but I fell for Howard so hard that when I flew to Johns Hopkins after the show, while I was in my room waiting to be seen by the doctor, I sat down and I wrote Howard a six-page love letter. I sent it care of Gary Dell'Abate on the show. I never did get a response, but I also never give up hope.

Life Now

I've had many long-term relationships and been engaged twice, but I never did marry or have any kids. I don't know…life is too short and I wish to God I would not have gone through my cocaine phase because I definitely think I would have accomplished more in my life. I think that I would have enjoyed more how everyone used to tell me how beautiful I was. But I was so high and just busy partying with rock stars and hanging out and having a great time instead of getting my life together.

I look back on my pictures and realize, "Wow. I really *was* beautiful." Guys would say, "Can I pinch you, are you real?" I thought it was a line at the time, but now I just really wish I had taken the time to enjoy my youth a little bit more and enjoy my beauty.

I imagine if I did all the things I did sober I probably would have enjoyed it a hell of a lot more. And there were so many times that I came close to doing some really stupid things that I am lucky to be alive today.

I just lost my mom to cancer, which is very hard. It's probably the most difficult thing I have ever endured. There are no words to express how much I miss her, but I know that I have to keep going. My mother and I were inseperable; we were best friends. I know she's watching over me right now, and that gives me comfort. I am very close to receiving my father's Oscar, which was left in his will to agent Marty Baum. I will be thrilled to have a tangible piece of my father with me in my home. My mother, I know, is always with me.

I am thrilled with the *Desperate Housewives* phenomenon because it's given women in their thirties and forties a chance to make a comeback. I've been spending time in the recording studio, and I've just recorded a mid-tempo dance single and plan to test the waters in Europe with it. I'm looking for a record producer to work with me and guide my career—because I will keep going until I hear myself singing on the radio. Singing is my passion, it's in my heart and soul, and I will never give up on my dream. My idols—Madonna, Mariah Carey, Janet Jackson, Cher and Britney Spears—got me through some serious heartache in my life. Now it's my turn. I'm taking everything one day at time, but things are looking great.

I just finished producing a documentary about my father with James Caan, Sydney Pollack, Shirley Jones, Dominick Dunne and a bunch of other big-name stars. I'm also just finishing writing my family's story. It's an incredible saga: sex, drugs, rock-and-roll, real estate, movie stars…everything. I want to do this project as a tribute to my mother, so everyone will know what a wonderful person she was. This project is very near and dear to my heart, as I worked on it for many years, even while I was in a wheelchair.

I also just finished writing a movie. It's about a boy who is born into unfortunate circumstances. He starts out as a murderer but turns into a serial killer. It's filled with sex, drama, religion…I threw everything in there. The reason I actually did it is because an ex-boyfriend of mine produced a movie called *Freeway* with Kiefer Sutherland and Reese Witherspoon. After I finished watching it and I saw his name at the end, I thought to myself, "I can write a movie better than that." So I called him and we talked and I told him my idea. Cut to five years later and he wants it.

I'm very talented—I'm a great producer, I'm a great writer, I'm a great singer. And I'm so happy to be healthy again that I feel like I can conquer the world. I find that I look and feel my best when I'm on the Zone-la.com diet—which is really necessary these days because I'm so busy. After everything I've been through I'm feeling more optimistic than ever about the future.